THE AI DILEMMA

THE  AI
DILEMMA

7 Principles for Responsible Technology

JULIETTE POWELL
AND ART KLEINER

Berrett–Koehler Publishers, Inc.

Berrett-Koehler Publishers, Inc.
1333 Broadway, Suite 1000
Oakland, CA 94612-1921
Tel: (510) 817-2277
Fax: (510) 817-2278
www.bkconnection.com

ORDERING INFORMATION

Quantity sales. Special discounts are available on quantity purchases by corporations, associations, and others. For details, contact the "Special Sales Department" at the Berrett-Koehler address above.

Individual sales. Berrett-Koehler publications are available through most bookstores. They can also be ordered directly from Berrett-Koehler: Tel: (800) 929-2929; Fax: (802) 864-7626; www.bkconnection.com.

Orders for college textbook / course adoption use. Please contact Berrett-Koehler: Tel: (800) 929-2929; Fax: (802) 864-7626.

Distributed to the U.S. trade and internationally by Penguin Random House Publisher Services.

Berrett-Koehler and the BK logo are registered trademarks of Berrett-Koehler Publishers, Inc.

Printed in the United States of America

Berrett-Koehler books are printed on long-lasting acid-free paper. When it is available, we choose paper that has been manufactured by environmentally responsible processes. These may include using trees grown in sustainable forests, incorporating recycled paper, minimizing chlorine in bleaching, or recycling the energy produced at the paper mill.

Library of Congress Cataloging-in-Publication Data

Names: Powell, Juliette, 1976- author. | Kleiner, Art, author.
Title: The AI dilemma : 7 principles for responsible technology / Juliette Powell
  and Art Kleiner.
Description: First edition. | Oakland, CA : Berrett-Koehler Publishers, Inc., [2023] |
  Includes bibliographical references and index.
Identifiers: LCCN 2023000959 (print) | LCCN 2023000960 (ebook) | ISBN
  9781523004195 (paperback) | ISBN 9781523004201 (pdf) | ISBN 9781523004218
  (epub) | ISBN 9781523004225 (audio)
Subjects: LCSH: Business—Technological innovations. | Artificial Intelligence—Moral
  and ethical aspects.
Classification: LCC HD45 .P659 2023 (print) | LCC HD45 (ebook) | DDC 330.0285/63—
  dc23/eng/20230310
LC record available at https://lccn.loc.gov/2023000959
LC ebook record available at https://lccn.loc.gov/2023000960

First Edition

31 30 29 28 27 26 25 24 23   10 9 8 7 6 5 4 3 2 1

Book production: Westchester Publishing Services
Cover design: Adam Johnson

To the community who inspired us to see the future: John Perry Barlow, Napier Collyns, George Geo Mueller, Dave Andre, Ivo Stivorik, Jonathan Askin, Ron Dembo, Jim Gellert, Helen Greiner, Che Marville, Astro Teller, Amelia Rose Barlow, and all of the Gatherists, as well as Stewart Brand, Ivan Illich, Alan Kay, Edie Seashore, J. Baldwin, and Pierre Wack

Contents

Foreword

How can you write a foreword for a book on artificial intel-ligence (AI) without descending into platitudes and obvious warnings about the dangers of AI—and solutions that would be great if people followed them?

AI is not a separate thing that humanity needs to fear. It's an expression of the very parts of humanity itself that we need to fear. Indeed, AI creates scalability and power for whoever uses it . . . and it empowers machines that follow orders in a way that at least some brave humans can resist.

So how can I be useful here? To start, I propose that we see AI as a way of discovering and fixing our imperfections rather than repeating and scaling them. Perhaps the cardinal recom-mendation in this book is to avoid the closed box. This ultimately means not just understanding AI but understanding people, who are also (mostly) closed boxes. People cannot effectively ex-plain most of their decisions even as they try to justify them.

So, if AI seems biased, look at the human models it is follow-ing. Indeed, AI is very good at discovering what's wrong in human society . . . and pointing at the solutions. For example, don't simply use AI to hire more people from "disadvantaged" backgrounds but go upstream and figure out how to fix those backgrounds. AI can help us to understand—and to persuade others to understand—the likely impact of fixing schools and paying teachers and caregivers wages that reflect their long-term value to society, rather than focusing on the amount parents and care-receivers can afford to pay in the short term.

With AI, we can get much better at discovering the counterfactuals and how much investment in schools, training, childcare, and the like could overcome those politely described "disadvantages." AI's ability to model things clearly—and to describe a range of outcomes—can help us analyze and manage our personal and our collective choices.

Back to the book!

Specifically, I love the way this book divides the exercise of power into four "logics"—those of engineers, society/activists, government/regulators, and corporations—as it looks at seven specific issues. They all make models, and they all make decisions according to their own perspectives. But there's another dimension missing, and that is time.

Even as AI makes it easier to predict the outcomes of certain actions—or inaction—society has become increasingly focused on short-term results. In so many ways, we are renting our future from an absentee landlord. No one is investing in our collective assets: physical infrastructure, environment, human capital. Even the government focuses on the short term: whatever will get votes. People are notoriously short-term in their thinking (ask Daniel Kahneman!), as are corporations (next-quarter earnings take precedence), while society is often divided or conflicted.

But I see hope, perhaps surprisingly, in one part of the corporate sector. Perhaps reinsurance companies could enter the fray and spread their long-term approach. The insurance industry has done great things to increase fire safety, automobile safety, and the like by establishing safety rules and inspecting their observance. In essence, insurance companies do not simply insure against risk. They reduce risk by forcing investment in security, durability, and risk reduction, for which they charge a carefully calculated premium. Imagine insuring the health of a population or the safety of a geography in this way. Humans and the other four quadrants undervalue the future, but reinsurance companies are in the business of improving outcomes and collecting the upfront funding to do so. And they are a bit more agile than governments, able to change their calculations and requirements in response to new data and outcomes.

My advice is not to let them rule but to let them price, protect, and invest in a better future in a way that the four quadrants cannot.

One way or another, this model is one of the best uses of AI. It will incentivize and force us to make decisions that do not discount the future—decisions for which we will be grateful later. With good AI-based counterfactuals, we will know exactly how grateful we should be.

Esther Dyson
Founder, Wellville, and longtime tech/
health investor/philanthropist

Preface

The story of how my great-aunt died gave me pause, and all the more so as I was doing the research that would fuel this book. During the pandemic, many governments used algorithms for triage purposes. Some countries used predictive modeling to assess how the contagion would spread, which groups of people were most vulnerable, and how governments should behave to diminish the death toll. Algorithms helped determine whether people should keep six feet, five feet, or three feet apart and whether their neighborhood would be quarantined. In some instances, the technology determined whether borders would be closed or remain open. The algorithmic decision making included how the hospitalized would be treated and who was expendable.

When the pandemic hit, my great-aunt, like many others, was in a retirement home. She did not make the cut for being treated like a person. She died alone, a 90-year-old nonperson, unable to understand what was happening or to communicate with anyone in the outside world. She was stuck in the system.

Thanks to COVID quarantines, she no longer had a phone. The nurses stopped answering when we called and soon thereafter stopped returning phone messages. People were dying alone, and the staff were overwhelmed. Even the caregiving staff that my great-aunt knew were now unrecognizable behind their masks and unable to provide the simplest of human comforts in the gift of laughter and a warm touch.

How horrifying and terrifying must that have been?

Thinking about that dehumanizing experience, I realized that my great-aunt was one of the lucky ones. All of the decisions that had led to her death were still made by humans.

In the future, we may turn these decisions over to machines. Would you want a piece of technology, intelligent or not, determining whether you made the cutoff for triage in a life-and-death situation? Would you want an artificial intelligence (AI) system determining whether or not to keep you on life support? Most technologists I spoke with don't even trust their own code, let alone someone else's code, to run their lives.

As my friend 3ric Johanson reminded me, humans have felt uncomfortable about artificial intelligence for as long as it's been around. Our best guess is that this discomfort stems from two fears: (1) AI might make decisions which we do not agree with (don't unplug my great-aunt!), and (2) AI is actually better than us at many tasks.

As a species we are slow to trust things we do not understand. We label serious versions of this feeling as "existential crisis." Advice from highly-trained professionals is likely to be listened to even less when delivered by AI. History is filled with examples of fear of what people cannot see or understand easily, including deities, germs, radiation, medicine, aliens, and now, AI. The more we evolve into a data-centric world, the harder it will be for these complex interdependent systems to be truly understood by trained professionals, let alone by everyday people. We should strive to integrate technology safely into our lives. At the same time, automated systems have no feelings, and we should be cautious about assuming they should.

Juliette Powell

Introduction

Machines That Make Life-or-Death Choices

Imagine you have to make a life-or-death choice in a matter of seconds. You're responsible for a self-driving car with sudden brake failure. It is careening forward with two possible paths. You have to decide, under pressure, who lives and who dies in a succession of scenarios: Three homeless people, or a doctor and an executive? Children or elderly people? Humans or pets? Jaywalkers or law-abiding street-crossers? Pregnant or nonpregnant women? Hit a barrier and kill the passenger, or hit a pedestrian in the crosswalk?

What's the best choice?

More than 2.3 million people from 233 countries have volunteered to answer these questions since the MIT Media Lab first posted the Moral Machine experiment in 2016. It is the largest online experiment in moral psychology ever created—an experience that invites people to choose the right ethical path for a powerful vehicle enabled by artificial intelligence.[1]

The Moral Machine is built on the trolley problem, the well-known thought experiment introduced by philosopher Philippa Foot in 1967.[2] In all of its many variations, some people must live, others must die, and there is limited time to choose. Media Lab faculty member Iyad Rahwan chose that problem as a way to test people's attitudes about self-driving cars. Rahwan and his fellow researchers wanted to explore the psychological road-blocks that might keep people from using these vehicles or other AI systems. To realize their potential value in reducing traffic congestion, augmenting safety, and cutting greenhouse gas emissions, the public must accept, purchase, and use these vehicles. This experiment would illuminate the barriers to acceptance.

The MIT researchers would have been happy to attract 500 participants: enough to make the results statistically significant. But the thought experiment struck a nerve. The preeminent journal *Science* and the *New York Times* published articles on the Moral Machine and included links to the site.[3] On the day the *Science* article appeared, two MIT graduate students behind the simulation, Edmond Awad and Sohan Dsouza, had to fly from Boston to Chicago for a conference. By the time their two-hour flight landed, Rahwan was already calling them frantically. About 100,000 people had visited the website at the same time and the unexpected traffic crashed the server. Awad and Dsouza had to relaunch the site during the taxi ride to their hotel, using a smartphone as a Wi-Fi hotspot.[4]

The experiment continued to go viral, off and on, during the next few years. Popular gaming commentators like PewDiePie and jacksepticeye posted YouTube videos of themselves playing this moral dilemma game, with 5 million and 1.5 million views, respectively. People discussed it on the front page of Reddit.[5] One reason for the experiment's growing popularity was un-doubtedly the ongoing news coverage of fatal accidents with self-driving cars. A Tesla Model S killed a passenger in February 2016 when it collided with a tractor-trailer truck in Williston, Florida. An Uber autonomous vehicle (AV) struck a woman walking her bicycle across a road in Tempe, Arizona in March 2018. There have been more such fatal crashes—11 just in the United States between May and September 2022.[6]

The Moral Machine results show that as artificial intelligence and automated systems become part of everyday life, they are forcing people to think about risk and responsibility more generally. In the experiment, millions of people expressed deeply held opinions about who should be sacrificed: children or adults, women or men, rich or poor? We rarely ask these questions of human drivers, but people want to think them through when AI is at the wheel.

As the authors of this book, we decided to do the experiment ourselves, responding to 13 horrific scenarios. As a former coder working on amphibious cars, Juliette took it very seriously, as if the responses really did mean life or death. Art felt more detached. To him, it was like playing a 1980s-era computer game with its simple graphics—but there was an unexpected gut punch. The site asked three questions at the end: Do you believe that your decisions on Moral Machine will be used to program actual self-driving cars? (*Probably not,* he thought. He doubted that the automakers would listen.) To what extent do you feel you can trust machines in the future? (After doing the experiment, he trusted them less.) To what extent do you fear that machines will become out of control? (The answer seemed much more complicated to him now.)

Taking the Trolley Problem to Scale

"Never in the history of humanity have we allowed a machine to autonomously decide who should live and who should die, in a fraction of a second, outside of real-time supervision," wrote Awad, Rahwan, and colleagues in their 2018 *Nature* article looking back at the experiment. "We are going to cross that bridge any time now, and it will not happen in a distant theater of military operations; it will happen in that most mundane aspect of our lives: everyday transportation. Before we allow our cars to make ethical decisions, we need to have a global conversation to express our preferences to the companies that will design moral algorithms, and to the policymakers that will regulate them. The Moral Machine was deployed to initiate such a conversation, and millions of people weighed in from around the world."[7]

"Never in the history of humanity have we allowed a machine to autonomously decide who should live and who should die, in a fraction of a second, outside of real-time supervision."

—Iyad Rahman, Edmund Awad, et al.

The results of that global conversation were sobering. Among all of those respondents, making 40 million decisions in 10 languages, there were only three universal preferences. Nearly everyone wanted to spare more lives rather than fewer lives. Almost all respondents favored humans over pets. They also preferred children over adults. That was it, except for a weak but still-evident general preference for saving the lives of pregnant women.

Beyond that, there is no consensus and there are strong contradictions. Respondents in many Asian countries say the elderly should be spared before the young. Residents of French-heritage countries and Latin America say the opposite. People in countries like the United States, with high gross domestic product

(GDP) per capita, prefer to save law-abiding pedestrians over jay-walkers. The opposite is true for people in places with lower GDP. A high Gini coefficient, which indicates a major gap between rich and poor, correlates with wanting to save wealthy pedestrians over unhoused people. The opposite is true for countries with a high social safety net. There are strong disagreements about saving groups that look like families with two adults and children, versus saving doctors and business leaders.

The Moral Machine is still online, and it still taps a nerve. People are attracted to it, in part, because they realize that self-driving vehicles—and other automated systems—are increasingly in widespread use. They are powerful, accessible, easy to use, and appear to give us what we want.

Our values often don't align. How, then, can we expect AI to know what priorities to control for, and whose interests to look after?

The Moral Machine, however, shows that people—especially those in different countries, cultures, and contexts—don't agree on what we want. We all control for different priorities. Our values often don't align. How, then, can we expect AI to know what priorities to control for and whose interests to look after—not just in life-and-death situations, but everywhere?

The Purpose of This Book

A turning point occurred as we were finishing *The AI Dilemma*. New digital tools—mostly based on natural language processing (NLP) systems and deep learning models, and trained on large learning models (LLMs)—were released in rapid succession to the public. These generative AI programs include apps like DALL-E, ChatGPT, and GPT-4 from OpenAI, along with natural language search engines from Microsoft and Google.

Suddenly, it is easy to create and alter images, text, and interactive media within seconds. Millions of people have shared their assisted creations through social media.[8] It is clear that these new tools are already changing habits.[9]

Some creative people regard the new AI systems as threatening. "These generators are created using thefted artwork, and in turn, undervalue the work of the original artists," wrote La'Kay Hodge, a creator of visual, written, and interactive work currently at NYU's Interactive Telecommunications Program. "We can understand the ethics of not stealing art and claiming it as our own, but for some reason, if a machine does it, not a word is uttered to stop it."[10]

Others find the technology absorbing and liberating. "It is only recently that AI has been accused of harming artists," said 3ric Johanson, whose title is Entropy Generator at Intellectual Ventures Laboratory. "I've heard arguments that it should be unethical for AI to be able to see other people's artwork in order to make derivative works; yet this is the exact function artists use for their inspiration. Future artists are those that can glitch the matrix and neural networks to make new styles and expressive design."[11]

We heard many different opinions about the value, promise, and dangers of AI while researching this book, and there was one common thread: the technology is here to stay. Writer Kevin Kelly cautioned us that the movement toward restricting AI "is biased toward protecting humans and I am much more interested in liberating machines."[12] Yes, the development of artificial intelligence will continue to progress, and that will be an enormous benefit—perhaps essential to civilization in the future. At the same time, Kelly is in the category of people who, historically, have been least likely to be harmed. These systems consistently raise significant, complex problems that will not simply resolve themselves. That's why having more diversity of thought and perspective, weighing in on these matters that affect all of us, is so important.

We can't live with automated systems, and we can't live without them. As our friend Helene Spierman put it, "The technology in the wrong hands is dangerous but in the right hands is beneficial to all." This is the AI dilemma. A way through this dilemma is the subject of this book.

We assigned ourselves three tasks:

1. Explore this dilemma and its implications.
2. Show how the technology is not separate from the people who make it or use it. The responsibility for its use, abuse, and oversight is shared among us all.
3. Help us use these tools to gain real control in our lives instead of just the illusion of control.

This is not a technical book. It does not explain the technical ways in which machine learning can be used or designed. It is also not a technology-bashing book, or a book about industrial policy or geopolitical supremacy through AI. We focus on how decision makers can think more clearly and act more effectively.

We use the term "artificial intelligence" throughout *The AI Dilemma* because that's the term generally recognized by the public. The term is misleading, however, because it implies similarity to human intelligence. Automated software processes are not intelligent. Engineers prefer the term "machine learning." We also use the phrase "Triple-A systems" to refer to related software technologies: algorithmic, autonomous, and automated systems.[13]

Triple-A systems are adaptive, which means that they change based on experience and data. That's how they train themselves. Triple-A systems are autonomous; once trained, they don't need a human to supervise them. Even in complex situations, they can perform tasks without people watching over them.

The Triple-A systems we care about most are sociotechnical systems. Their design and performance depend just as much on human and social elements as on the technology. We can only understand and improve them if we treat each AI system as an integrated, interdependent whole: a complex system comprising machines, people, and organizations.

Some people fear that Triple-A systems will replace human judgment or overtake human agency. Instead, they have become a forcing function, changing the way we pay attention to ourselves. If people can't tell the difference between disinformation and information, if we can't discern between guidance from a chatbot and from another human, and if we can't connect meaningfully in a flood of AI-enabled content, then what does that say about us?

The Illusion of Control

When Harvard psychologist Ellen Langer coined the phrase "the illusion of control" back in the 1970s, she was studying gambling and addiction. Meeting her, you would probably be impressed by her outspoken, sharp manner and her overall joie de vivre.[14] It is no surprise, then, that she could talk with anyone about their feelings. Langer chose to focus on gamblers to shape a hypothesis on feelings of control. It turns out that when gamblers feel their own skill is involved, they expect to have a higher success rate than statistical probability would warrant in a game of chance.

Based on these results, she predicted that elements of competition, choice, familiarity, and engagement, when designed into games of chance, would cause people to feel overly confident.[15]

Even though the study dates back to 1975, Langer's conclusions still hold. Gambling has evolved over time to encourage people to feel more confident about winning. For example, state lotteries allow people to pick their own lottery numbers. This provides them with a false sense that they actually have control over which number wins the stake. Studies of slot machines have similarly found that some features are included explicitly to give players a sense of control. For example, near-misses generate the "winning" sound of coins dropping, and the stop button lets users halt the spinning of the wheels, which has only a random effect on the outcome. The desire for control is a strong element of gambling addiction.[16]

The same is true of many Triple-A systems, most notoriously in social media. Former Facebook president Sean Parker has been very vocal about the deliberately addictive nature of the algorithms for these systems. They were designed to exploit what he calls the "vulnerability in human psychology,"[17] which refers to the desire to feel in control of the situation. The same is true of many digital games and gamified e-commerce sites. Advancing a level in a game or using a one-click button provides a physical satisfaction associated in the brain with having more control. The craving that these systems exploit appears to be biological, universal, and hardwired. We all have a deep need to feel in control of our lives, and it may be rooted in "a biological imperative for survival."[18]

When we asked neuroscientists about this need for control and its possible relationship to Triple-A systems, nearly every reply led us back to the same paper: "Born to Choose: The Origins and Value of the Need for Control," which was published in 2011 by three researchers at Columbia University in New York. Psychology professor Kevin Ochsner is known for his research on cognitive neuroscience, emotional control, and attitude change. Lauren Leotti was then a graduate student and is now on the psychology faculty at Rutgers University. We ended up interviewing the other author, management professor Sheena Iyengar, whose book *The Art of Choosing* further expands on this idea.

Based on their broad survey of neuroscience imaging research, including research on people with Alzheimer's disease and schizophrenia, Leotti, Iyengar, and Ochsner link this craving for control to the medial prefrontal cortex. This area of the brain is associated with making choices and taking control. As Iyengar put it, people are biologically wired to "being causal agents, rather than passive observers." Put another way: "The desire for control is an essential part of what it means to be human."[19]

Many people with an affinity for technology have the sense that we are in control of our devices. We use them to make decisions and execute tasks more quickly and seamlessly than we otherwise could. With the guidance and prompts we get from responsive Triple-A systems, these decisions seem just as good, and probably better, than the decisions we would have made otherwise. For example, we might get in the habit of using GPS while driving, even if we know the route, because the guidance gives us the feeling of being more in control. The system might tell us, for instance, if there's a traffic accident or construction along the way—or just reassure us that we are on the right track to getting to work on time.

But deep down, we might also suspect that the technology could betray us at any moment. What if, as some psychology researchers suggest, our extensive use of GPS is causing our mind's innate spatial cognition capabilities to atrophy, like an unused muscle would? Can we really be sure that's not happening?[20] What if the GPS guidance system is actually directing us down a less optimal route because it needs to gather data about traffic conditions there? If a company did that, how would we ever know?[21] What if our credit card number or Social Security number ends up on the dark web because of a security breach at our phone carrier?

Three Steps Toward Real Control

If automated systems are actually manipulating our sensation of being in control while reducing our actual control, then one of the primary ways to reduce risk and harm in our automated world would be to increase our real control over our lives and our systems.

The first step would be coming to terms with the fact that much of our sense of control is illusory. We generally think we have more control than we actually do. Whether it's the social safety net, the corporate safety net, the economic safety net, or the support of other people, if we rely on it, we are vulnerable to it being taken away. We discover this when there's a crisis. For example, many people discovered during the pandemic that the external support of business, government, school, medicine and even family could not be there for them in the same way, or the way they needed it.

> With Chat-GPT, you might get into the habit of turning work in without even editing it. Over time, this illusory sensation could come to feel like real power.

The second step would be to see the impact of AI on our own feelings of control. You experience headiness when you tell Open-AI's Chat-GPT to write a paper based on three keywords, and it instantly produces something as good as what you might have written yourself. When that happens, you want to share that headiness with the world in terms of the output, the time saved, and the sheer effortlessness of "your accomplishment." You may feel that you're getting things done with far less friction. You might get into the habit of turning work in without even editing it. Over time, this illusory sensation could come to feel like real power.

The third step is learning to tell the difference between real control and the illusory feeling. Sheena Iyengar has dedicated much of her life to studying this and her primary indicator of real control is the difficulty you perceive. As she told us in our interview, "Being in genuine control is burdensome. Comparing different trade-offs takes effort." If you perceive there to be tough choices involved, requiring your attention and concentration, without a pleasant outcome, then it is probably genuine control. Real control often requires you to weigh the pros and cons of each option and take into account the short- and long-term consequences for each—especially if you care about the outcome.

Consider the Moral Machine experiment. Each decision involves a life-and-death trade-off. The game pushes you to make that decision quickly, but the stakes are low unless you choose to suspend disbelief. If those were real people, and you were speeding toward them with limited power to stop the car, you would agonize. That feeling of agony would be a signal of being in real control. As it is, the greatest level of real control in the experiment is the recognition that you probably don't have much influence over how the self-driving cars are programmed to make these life-and-death decisions.

Iyengar confirmed that real choice involves more effort when the outcome has meaning. "That's when you discover you have to pay attention after all," she said. "You may not really want to pay attention. You may think you want to make more choices in your life, but you often find out you don't actually like making real choices."[22]

Even if you are willing to make hard choices, people have only so much capacity for complex decision making in a day.[23] Iyengar says that the number of decisions that people make today is much greater than it was, say, 50 years ago. For example, in the 1960s, the average US citizen married someone who lived within a four-block radius. In 2013, there were an estimated 8,000 dating and matchmaking apps in the world, with about 2,500 in the United States alone.[24] It's natural for people to delegate their decisions about navigation to Triple-A systems because we only have the capacity to process a few of the thousands of decisions we make daily.

What Comes Next

We designed *The AI Dilemma* to help you become more aware of the difference between control and the illusion of control—and to put that awareness to use. Here is a quick overview of the chapters:

Chapter 1: Four Logics of Power. Four main perspectives influence AI, often at cross-purposes.

The next four chapters describe principles that apply to Triple-A systems. We derived them through four years of research at Columbia University and subsequent interviews.

Chapter 2: Be Intentional about Risk to Humans. Think in terms of costs and benefits to make sure short-term gains do not put others—or your reputation—at risk.

Chapter 3: Open the Closed Box. Make AI explainable in a way that makes sense to each type of stakeholder. Be open about what you can and cannot reveal.

Chapter 4: Reclaim Data Rights for People. Empower everyone to control their personal information.

Chapter 5: Confront and Question Bias. Ensure that Triple-A outcomes are ethical and fair to everyone affected by them.

The principles in the next three chapters describe changes that are taking place in organizations and society to enable the first four principles.

Chapter 6: Hold Stakeholders Accountable. Set up practices that regulate Triple-A systems effectively.

Chapter 7: Favor Loosely Coupled Systems. Redesign AI teams and organizations to promote diverse thinking and flexible responses.

Chapter 8: Embrace Creative Friction. Create an environment of trust, thoughtfulness, and psychological safety to bring responsible AI into the future.

Our **Conclusion**, which returns to the Moral Machine, suggests that we can apply these principles and get to where we need to go as a global society. *It's not too late to start.*

Four Logics of Power

Biographer Walter Isaacson tells the story of Nobel Prize–winning biochemist Jennifer Doudna's earliest encounter with the topic of DNA research. She came home from sixth grade to find a paperback left by her father on her bed: *The Double Helix*, James Watson's first-person account of the discovery of DNA.[1] She thought at first the book was a detective story, and in a sense, it was: "She became enthralled by the intense drama behind the competition to discover the building blocks of life," wrote Isaacson. [2]

Doudna resolved to carry on with similar research, even though her high school guidance counselor told her girls didn't become scientists. In 2011, she and French microbiologist Emmanuelle Charpentier met at a conference and began their collaboration on developing a method for high-precision genome editing. "They turned their curiosity into an invention that will transform the human race," wrote Isaacson, "an easy-to-use tool that can edit DNA, known as CRISPR." They used the immune system of a bacterium, which disables viruses by cutting their DNA up with a type of genetic scissors. By extracting and simplifying the genetic scissors' molecular components, they made DNA editing and CRISPR a topic of global discussion and public debate. Doudna was among the first women to win a Nobel

Prize in science when, in 2020, she shared the prize in chemistry with Charpentier.[3]

"The CRISPR/Cas9 genetic scissors will probably lead to new scientific discoveries," says a Nobel Prize website summary, "better crops, and new weapons in the fight against cancer and genetic diseases."[4] The technology is also so dangerous that Doudna—along with other leading scientists in the field, including Charpentier—has publicly advocated to pause research until there is acceptable oversight.[5] Currently, 30 countries ban or severely restrict research on human germline gene modification, and the World Health Organization maintains a registry of projects.[6]

Doudna's position is noteworthy for its nuanced perspective. For example, in her seminal 2015 TED talk, she discussed the many benefits that CRISPR could provide, but she also raised the prospects of "designer babies" and the general loss of control over the technology that could stem from choices like eliminating human genetic diversity. The TED talk so far has received more than 4 million views.

"The opportunity to do this kind of genome editing," she said, "also raises various ethical issues that we have to consider. This technology can be employed not only in adult cells but also in the embryos of organisms, including our own species. And so, together with my colleagues, I've called for a global conversation about the technology that I coinvented, so that we can consider all of the ethical and societal implications of a technology like this."[7]

Clearly, there are precedents for global discussion and decision about the acceptable limits for emerging technologies. Other examples include human cloning, biological warfare, nuclear weapons—and, now, Triple-A systems. No agreement has completely halted a technology, but many dangers have been rethought or mitigated.

Just as *The AI Dilemma* is being edited, a wave of regulatory interest in responsible technology and Triple-A systems is rising. In September 2022, the United States White House released a proposed blueprint for an AI Bill of Rights.[8] Its five principles map onto principles that we had already identified in our research. You will see them at the front of five of our chapters. Similar principles appear in discussions leading up to the European Union's proposed new Artificial Intelligence Act (AIA).[9] A number of other frameworks for AI responsibility have been put forth, going back to 2018 or earlier.[10]

What these frameworks seem to have in common, at least implicitly, is that each takes into account four logics of power related to Triple-A systems—corporate, engineering, government, and social justice (see figure 1). Just as Jennifer Doudna wanted people from different backgrounds to participate in the CRISPR

	Private	Public
Individual	**Engineering logic** Technology	**Social justice logic** Humanity
Institutional	**Corporate logic** Ownership, markets, and growth	**Government logic** Authority and security

FIGURE 1   The Four Logics of Power
Source: Kleiner Powell International (KPI).

conversation and not just scientists, these four logics of power each represent a different priority and way of thinking about the issues. As an individual, you may relate to one of these perspectives more than the others, but none of them are inherently right or wrong. Together, they give us a sense of the possibilities and tensions that arise in finding solutions that work for all of us.

The Engineering Logic: The Perspective of Technologists

A highly skilled and in-demand computer or systems engineer working on AI is analytical, fast, and "efficient." A highly-valued AI engineer can translate ideas into software or hardware. She communicates as an engineer on behalf of other similarly trained engineers, as well as on behalf of the algorithm, the Triple-A system, the organizational goals, and the client. In some cases, she also communicates on behalf of the user.

We spoke with multiple systems engineers who do not, within their organizational roles, think or communicate on behalf of end users. Engineers refer to the mind-set or culture of engineering as having three priorities. The first priority is to the customer, the company that buys or licenses the technology. Engineers report being "customer-obsessed." The second priority is the technical challenge of an "interesting problem" that they and "only a handful of others in the world" can solve. Engineers value being part of a technical community of dedicated, highly-skilled analytic specialists who understand one another. The third priority may be the individuals (us) who will interact with or be affected by the product, depending on the engineer.[11]

That's just "engineers being engineers," according to Casey Cerretani, an AI systems engineer and executive who has done everything from inventing and customizing new servers to running teams of hundreds of developers at several prominent Big Tech companies. In his role, he is the connection between the customer, the company providing the tech, and all the engineers working on the project. In his own words: "The task is to do the thing that the customer is asking for." Everything else might be considered "noise" because in the face of solving a pressing complex problem, it "doesn't matter." Everything else is not technically their job.[12]

Engineers like Cerretani see the larger context and implications of their work on things like privacy but are driven by the technical requirements of the customer. The user is not viewed as their problem—the end user is not the customer.

Instead, end user responsibility is delegated to other areas of the firm like user interface design, marketing, PR, "corporate social responsibility," customer service, "HR," and legal departments. Some technologists feel personally involved with considerations of AI responsibility, especially if they have been personally affected by negative outcomes from AI. They see the problems more keenly than non-engineers do. They may then apply the same analytic perspective to finding solutions. If they recognize that technology on its own won't suffice, they may try to change or influence their organizations by speaking out. Then they discover the hard way how resistant corporate logic can be to whistleblowing or direct confrontation. One example is Tristan Harris from the Center for Humane Technology, a former Googler who has been outspoken about the tech's effect on people in talks, interviews, and his own popular podcast under the TED audio umbrella.[13]

The Social Justice Logic: The Perspective of Humanity

This logic upholds a people-first sensibility; it prioritizes the social contract. People count more for this group than efficiency, profit, security, and control. When these other priorities take supremacy over people's human rights, the social justice logic pushes back in the form of community organizing, walkouts, petitions, data leaks, whistleblowing, media attacks, and public discourse. From the social justice perspective, the only way to truly gain legitimacy for AI is to make it responsible to all stakeholders, especially those who have been marginalized in the past, and to give all stakeholders a voice.

> *"Right now, the burden is on us, the public, to prove that these algorithms harm us. I want that burden to be on the companies who profit from using them."*
>
> —Cathy O'Neil

As community leaders, social justice advocates make it their business to be keenly aware of issues that need improvement. Cathy O'Neil, data scientist and author of *Weapons of Math Destruction* and *The Shame Machine*, put it this way: "Right now, the burden is on us, the public, to prove that these algorithms harm us. I want that burden to be on the companies who profit from using them."[14]

Some of the systems engineers we interviewed are deeply motivated by this logic. We were told by several people in Big Tech that conversations about this juxtaposition of social justice logic and the logic of corporate and engineering efficiency "never happen" within the firm. You might expect that because some systems engineers report to the CEO or CFO of their organizations that they could discuss any concerns directly with the C-suite. But sadly, there is a pervasive gap in communication when it comes to conflicting moral and corporate values. For example, when asked explicitly if he ever thinks about how the technology he creates will be deployed, Cerretani distinguishes between his personal feelings about social justice and the logic of the firms he serves: "You can quickly imagine all the black hat ways that [Triple-A systems] could be used, which could be viewed as nefarious. That certainly challenges me. But there's not much of an organizational conversation around that. And I think that's the big missing gap. It is as much an ethical conversation as it is a technological one."

"You can quickly imagine all the black hat ways that [Triple A's] could be used, which could be viewed as nefarious. But there's not much of an organizational conversation around that. And I think that's the big missing gap."

—Casey Cerretani

There are many social justice activists connected to the AI community—either from having worked there, or from independent work. Their insider knowledge enriches the context through which they talk about social justice and adds to their proficiency and impact. For example, Dan Gillmor, tech journalist and director of the News Co/Lab at Arizona State University, is also a board member of the Signals Network, a nonprofit that supports whistleblowers and connects them to journalism organizations.[15]

The Corporate Logic: The Logic of Ownership, Markets, and Growth

One reason for the gap in corporate conversation is what Casey Cerretani calls "the gung-ho race to get the technology in place" in most companies. "Microsoft Cloud Services is growing at 70 plus percent, year over year. Amazon is growing at a similar rate. Those are very large percentages on very large baseline numbers. When you grow that quickly and you're growing to meet these customer needs, you don't go back and do a lot of housekeeping."

By "housekeeping," Cerretani means any concern for the harmful impact of the technology on vulnerable populations. The conflict between engineering, social justice, and corporate logics leads many companies to intensify secrecy so that their leaders don't have to confront or resolve the clash of values. These conflicts are coming to a head within many organizations today, but meaningful conversations about them are missing from corporate life because they would slow down the "gung-ho" rush to produce results.

"There are just three cloud service providers for the whole world. Maybe two of them will emerge as the winners in the end. That's an enormous power."

—Casey Cerretani

We have all seen corporate leaders making decisions to enhance shareholder value. It is their job. As a result, the corporate logic represents a logic of power. It prioritizes money, profit growth, expansion, new business, and dominance over competitors. "There are just three cloud service providers for the whole world," Cerretani reminds us. "Maybe two of them will emerge as the winners in the end. That's an enormous power."

And if you have got shares in either of those companies, lucky you.

Corporate logic is inherently narrow. Corporate leaders often think of themselves as broadminded, but as Cerretani says, "You have a corporate mission. You have a corporate direction. You have customers. And it becomes an interesting slippery slope."[16] Warnings that don't fit the perceived immediate customer needs get lost as they travel up the official channels. In many technical teams, for example, graphic specialists create the data visualizations, and thus the PowerPoint messages that reach the C-suite. They may only describe the aspects that they think sponsors want to hear about.

When everyone makes decisions based on what they think the top leaders and customers expect, the outcomes are risky. With Triple-A systems, the risk is greatest for vulnerable populations. It may also extend to engineers and other employees, and might ultimately lead some corporations themselves to fall. Those who want to restrain the risk tend to turn to another logic of power: the logic of government.

Government Logic: The Perspective of Authority and Security

In the government logic, no matter which country or system, two things are paramount: governments protect the nation or jurisdiction from outside forces, and they provide support and public service for their citizens. From this standpoint, Triple-A technology is something for public sector organizations to use, invest in, regulate—and possibly to develop themselves.

Politicians are concerned about AI because they are vulnerable to automated systems that manipulate public opinion. The government logic thus sees regulation as inevitable. That is, there needs to be standards governing the use of Triple-A technology, even if politicians and regulators have a wide range of views of what the standards should be.

The government logic is further complicated by the fact that AI systems can be used by politicians to attack their competitors. The same digital tools that enable human trafficking are also used to uncover and arrest traffickers and to find lost people. AI also gives the government itself more capabilities in everything it does, including the regulation of citizens. At the same time, to paraphrase free software activist John Gilmore,[17] automated systems interpret regulation as damage and route around it.

For Cerretani, the job of regulating companies is squarely the responsibility of the government. Many would agree. The burden is on governments everywhere to resolve the paradox of the AI dilemma. Government leaders may be increasingly measured by their ability to use this powerful technology judiciously. If they overreach, it may be obvious to outsiders in ways their leaders did not anticipate. They may have to demonstrate that they are fair and accountable to all citizens. They may also have to encourage innovation even as they require innovators to limit what they do.

All Together Now

When we each learn to appreciate and understand the other logics, it builds an overall level of trust. That in turn makes the whole Triple-A ecosystem more trustworthy.

None of the four logics are in control. There are no right or wrong answers. If we want trustworthy AI systems, we need to bring all four perspectives together, keep them in mind simultaneously, and make the effort to understand why others feel and think the way they do. The point is to use all four logics together to better evaluate our systems in each use case and context. Then we're much more likely to create systems that work for more people.

In the next chapter, we introduce the first of our seven principles: be intentional about risk to humans.

CHAPTER 2

Be Intentional about Risk to Humans

You should be protected from unsafe or ineffective systems.

—Blueprint for an AI Bill of Rights

On the night of September 26, 1983, a 44-year-old Soviet Air Defense Forces lieutenant-colonel named Stanislav Petrov was on duty monitoring a Soviet satellite-based missile tracking system when an alarm sounded. The system showed that five American intercontinental ballistic missiles were heading toward the Soviet Union from the United States. Petrov was trained to report the warning signal immediately to his commanding officer. Instead, he responded to his own "gut instinct," as he later put it, and sent a report saying the alarm was a system malfunction.

Petrov considered the detection a computer error since a first-strike nuclear attack by the United States would have likely involved hundreds of simultaneous missile launches in order to disable any Soviet means of a counterattack. Furthermore, the satellite system's reliability had been questioned in the past.[1]

Petrov's gut instinct was right. It was a malfunction. The US had sent no missiles. The Soviets did not retaliate, and Petrov ended up being hailed as a hero by both sides in the Cold War.[2] Petrov single-handedly stopped the automated machine of nuclear holocaust.

How I Learned to Stop Worrying and Love AI

On September 26, 2022—the 39th anniversary of Petrov's feat—we decided to add his story to the manuscript. The Russia-Ukraine war was raging on, and many people were afraid of nuclear weapon escalation. Surely, no country would put an algorithm in a role like Petrov's, where civilization was at stake?

To Art, no country would seriously abandon human oversight, replacing the likes of Petrov with a system. Curious to know what the experts would say, Juliette asked physicists and computer scientists—people who were familiar with the nexus of nuclear and artificial intelligence (AI)—if this future was plausible.

It turned out that these experts were worried too. So is the Bulletin of Atomic Scientists, the group cofounded by Albert Einstein.[3] The biggest concern we heard is not about the technology itself but about the way AI could be misused in a nuclear weapons context.

"There is a continuing push for increased automation [in nuclear weapons]," writes Marka Szabolcs, professor of physics at Columbia University. The cause, according to Szabolcs, is the ever-decreasing time available for decision making. "Automated systems shall inevitably include sophisticated AIs at all levels," he adds. "I sincerely hope that humans will never wake up to be wholly excluded from the loop. However, there are many military powers with markedly different philosophies competing worldwide. Some of them might decide that AI response times are a critical advantage. In a changing, chaotic, and globally competitive world, AI automated weapons of mass destruction are *a terribly scary eventuality.*" In other words, he said the use of AI to monitor and direct nuclear weapons response is not just a possibility. It will happen.[4]

You may be reading this and thinking that machine learning represents a different kind of risk than nuclear weapons, and we would agree. But perhaps not in the way you may think.

Triple-A systems are ubiquitous, woven deeply into daily life. Most of the effect is benign, but when there is risk, it is significant. You may already have felt some effects personally, like some of the people whose stories we learned about in our research for *The AI Dilemma.* Your data might have been exposed, making you vulnerable to identity theft, scams by simulated "friends," or stalking by a predator. You could be targeted by ads and videos that take advantage of your impulses. You or someone you know might have been tagged by a government's facial-recognition system and falsely accused of a crime. This is not an academic issue or a warning about some hypothetical possibility. The use of Triple-A systems has been particularly likely to lead to harsh and arbitrary outcomes for vulnerable populations, like children, minority groups, and women.

Predictive analytics are a major factor. When statistical averages suggest that someone is probably guilty of criminal behavior, or undeserving of credit, or likely to fail, the human systems tend to follow along. We don't realize how often this happens because the AI systems and their outcomes tend to be hidden from view.

Being intentional about risk means not just focusing on it when it's convenient, when the costs of reducing risk are low, or when it feels comfortable. It means continually looking for ways to achieve twin goals: deploying technology to realize its potential and reducing the potential harm to the people or communities where the technology is deployed.

Hedging Your Bets during Radical Uncertainty

A real-world example of the Moral Machine dilemma occurred late at night on a wide suburban road in Tempe, Arizona, in 2018, when an autonomous vehicle killed a 49-year-old woman named Elaine Herzberg. This was the first pedestrian death associated with self-driving technology. One of Uber's demonstration automated vehicles, a modified Volvo SUV, was traveling at 40 miles an hour. Herzberg was running with her bike to cross the road.[5]

According to risk management expert and entrepreneur Ron Dembo, who analyzed the case in his 2022 book *Risk Thinking*, "an experienced human driver might have reasoned (in milliseconds) that there [was] a scenario in which the object on the side of the road might be a living being that was about to cross. The driver would have 'hedged' their risk by slowing down to reduce the chances of a collision until they had gathered additional information."

"By the time the Uber vehicle recognized the object as a woman with a bike," writes Dembo, "it was too late. It had not reduced its speed, and at that point, if the woman decided to run across the road, there was going to be a collision—and it was almost surely going to be fatal. Perhaps neither the autonomous vehicle nor the operator had ever encountered a situation like this before. Still, if we are to have autonomous vehicles on the road, they need to be able to manage risks like these—they need to be able to strategize and make decisions even when presented with incomplete information."[6]

To Dembo, this was a case of inadequate risk thinking in the software design. By "risk thinking," he means the ability to take uncertainty into account, to choose a flexible path that can respond to events as they unfold. Stanislav Petrov was demonstrating risk thinking when he stopped nuclear war by diagnosing the system malfunction. The AI program in the Uber vehicle did not have risk thinking in its repertoire. When it did not recognize the type of motion it sensed, it did not have a programmed way of responding to uncertainty, so it kept up its speed until it was too late to avoid a collision. In a sense, Uber as a company also lacked risk thinking. This event forced it to suspend its testing of self-driving cars. They ultimately sold their self-driving division, which had been a key part of their business strategy.[7]

It is important to note there was a human operator in the car when the accident happened. Her job was not to drive, but to observe and report on the car's actions. During the few seconds before the accident occurred, she was looking down, and the car didn't alert her until less than a second before impact—at which point she grabbed the wheel.

This is an example of a frequent dynamic with automated systems, first discovered in the earliest days of pilot flight training. It's known as *automation complacency*. The more autonomous the machine, the more people tend to trust it and not pay full attention. As we get in the habit of not paying attention, we enter the *uncanny valley of automation*, a negative reinforcing loop. For pilots, the use of autopilot meant that their flying skills actually eroded. In general, the more automation, the less people pay attention. The less attention, the more accidents. The more accidents, the more demand for automation. The negative spiral continues.[8]

In Dembo's terms, the human beings delegate their own "risk thinking" to the machine, but the machine is not up to the task. That is what appeared to happen in Tempe.[9] Automation complacency continues to cause trouble everywhere people oversee automated technology. We wait and watch for days at a time, assigned to see a signal that something improbable but possible is happening. We get bored, grow complacent, and do not see it. Security guards suffer from this. The same goes for human agents looking after nuclear reactors, drones, and many Triple-A systems.

When Dembo spoke with us during his family trip to Costa Rica in 2022, he was careful to add that AI, in general, is improving its risk thinking capability. Even so, there is a long way to go. Dembo has a theory about times of radical uncertainty, when the butterfly effect is rampant,[10] and small events often lead to large crises. He says they put AI systems at a disadvantage, compared to people. "Humans are natural risk thinkers, generalizing from small amounts of data, trading off upside with downside and regret as we navigate through life. Every complex decision we make is our way of dealing with some future uncertain event, balancing risk and return, even if it is not explicit."[11]

An example of risk thinking in policy and business decision making is scenario planning. It is a management approach that involves considering multiple future possibilities. In a typical scenario exercise, you and your team see trouble ahead. You don't know what it is. A predictive algorithm would select only one approach and act on it. Instead, you conceive of several different scenarios. In the case of self-driving cars, maybe that motion is a woman crossing the road with a bicycle, and you are about to hit her. Maybe it's a deer. Maybe it's a shadow or glare on your car window. You don't try to predict the future, but you put on the brakes—not because it's the solution to the problem but because it is the most robust option in front of you. Since you don't know exactly what will happen next, you find some strategic action that will yield at least a pretty good result in all possible futures.

You might think that the automated nature of AI would make it good at managing risk, at least in the right use cases. However, systems cannot predict the future because they are trained only with historical data from the past. As soon as new variables or conditions on the ground are introduced, as with the Uber accident that killed Elaine Herzberg, the system's predictive capabilities diminish. It wasn't trained with that data. Depending on the use case, a person's life may hang in the balance.

As risk thinkers, we want to hedge our bets so that when unexpected events occur, we can pivot and move with them. The Uber accident shows what happens when we don't risk-think with intentionality. When we do, as we will discover with serial entrepreneur Helen Greiner, intentionality can help us think effectively about even the most harmful risks. It can help us plan for the long-term implications of what we are doing, and hedge against negative unintended consequences. That's how we lower and mitigate the risk of Triple-A systems.

Robots, Drones, and Risk Intentionality

When Juliette first met Robotics entrepreneur Helen Greiner on an estate outside Boston, she said her childhood goal continues to drive her choices. Greiner makes a living making robots that people buy, and that girls would want to hack into.

"It started back when I was 11," recalls Greiner, "and I saw *Star Wars* and fell in love with R2-D2. He wasn't just a machine, right? He had an agenda. He saved the universe. He had a personality and a lot of expression with his bleeps and flutes. Since that time, I've always wanted to make things that are more than machines. I went to MIT to learn how. I learned a lot of great engineering there, but they didn't really know how to build robots for the real world."[12]

> *"I saw Star Wars and fell in love with R2-D2. He wasn't just a machine, right? He had an agenda. He saved the universe. Since that time, I've always wanted to make things that are more than machines."*
>
> **—Helen Greiner**

Greiner was an intensely bright child. She didn't speak until after she hit puberty, because she was far ahead of most of the conversations around her. Then, as a teenager, she became interested in robotics, and all of that changed. In 1990, she and two fellow MIT AI Lab alumni founded iRobot, creating custom-made industrial and military robots and prototypes for space travel and some of the earliest robotic toys. Any risk from the devices was barely evident. Many of them were explicitly intended to reduce human risk in dangerous places like underwater oil and gas drilling platforms.

Along the way, iRobot's leaders kept fiercely exploring the elements of commercial success, especially as one of a very few small start-ups making hardware and software with very little venture capital at first. Then came Defense Advanced Research Projects Agency (DARPA) funding and venture capital. Greiner and her team introduced two robots. The Roomba was the first autonomous home vacuum cleaner; it sold a million units within its first four years. The PackBot was like a Roomba for bomb disposal. It is credited with disarming thousands of improvised bombs in Iraq and Afghanistan, all of which would otherwise have taken soldier and civilian lives.

"Once I was speaking at the War College," recalled Greiner, "and I was between two three-star generals on my right and a four-star general on my left. And I assumed everyone would want to go speak to them after the conference. But a lot of the soldiers came up to me and one guy I remember, he shook my hand and said, 'This PackBot saved 11 guys on one mission.'"[13]

Greiner was chair and president of iRobot until 2008, when she left to form another start-up: a drone manufacturer called CyPhy Works, founded on the premise that robots and people can share airspace at least as easily and productively as ground-space. She left CyPhy in 2017 for a position advising the US Army on robotics. In 2020, she joined Tertill, a start-up founded by a former iRobot engineer, which makes home gardening robots that prevent weed growth and fertilize soil.[14]

Greiner is the kind of charismatic woman who gets invited to the White House and to participate in the World Economic Forum. She speaks from the heart and promotes the continued use of highly innovative AI technology, including in military spheres. Her ongoing dedication to service reflects her lifelong determination and her years of experience in reducing human risk. They also reflect an awareness of the potential benefits and threats inherent in AI-powered robots and drones.

In a conversation published in *Foreign Affairs*, Greiner tackles the dilemma head-on:

A terrorist could buy a drone today and start planning an attack with it, and I think the only way we're actually going to catch that is with human intelligence. Terrorists aren't going to get drones from a company building them for commercial reasons. They're going to go to the hobby store and buy the ones that are already freely available if they want to pack them with explosives. I think it's a challenge. But you can do the same with a car, and you don't say, 'Well, we shouldn't sell cars because you can use them in a suicide attack.' All we have to do is figure out who's going to be doing it and try to stop it.[15]

To Greiner, intentionality around risk is key. It also seems to be important for many people who follow her and her career—she is continually asked about the risks inherent in her work.

When the Risks Are Unacceptable

Several years ago, data scientist and artist Lynn Cherny found herself working on an AI system for community management. Its purpose was to reduce risk. The host company was a European start-up with an unusual cybersecurity service. It used a scouring algorithm to search for offensive and harassing messages on its clients' social media sites and chat rooms. The algorithm posted statistics about the abusive messages on a private dashboard, so clients could remove the messages and block new ones from appearing. Cherny and two other staff members were responsible for building the system that flagged content for human review. "It was the subject matter that was of concern here," she says, "in particular related to child harm."[16]

Just the exposure to this type of content took a terrible toll on her team. In our interview with her from her home in France, Cherny said that some client sites were rife with abuse, trolling, and aggressive hate speech. "There was a lot of consensual sexting. But we also saw unsolicited obscene messages, or overly friendly stalking. We saw messages to underage people from predatory people, grooming them or asking for nude photos. There were also notes with suicidal ideation and a few threats of real-world violence."[17]

The most disturbing aspect, recounts Cherny, was the reaction of her managers when she suggested that the dashboard could filter for things like child grooming. Her managers didn't even want to discuss it with clients. "They said that if they followed my advice, the company would be legally liable." Some child harassment messages would inevitably slip through the filters, and if that came to light, the company would rather say it didn't know there were problem areas. "The bosses didn't want to know about anything awkward."

This meant, of course, that the predators and their messages would remain. The intentions were lost.

Cherny and one of her team members left the start-up soon after, citing multiple issues, including the depressing subject matter. "We asked ourselves: Should we even be looking for these things if the client doesn't care?" Regardless of their technological skills and the perception of control associated with their jobs, Cherny's team did not have the organizational clout to raise the issue further—and if the human moderators who are hired to reduce harm aren't in control, then who is?

We have heard similar stories from many others in Big Tech—in varied circumstances but generally with the same bleak outlook. Casey Cerretani says that technologists in roles like his regularly see evidence of sex trafficking—for example, by clients using servers they work on. It may bother engineers, but it is generally not their job to speak out, and there could be repercussions for even mentioning it. Circumstances like this, he says, make software engineers skeptical about trying to influence change from within. Instead, they try to make enough money to leave Big Tech to better invest in new start-ups that reflect their values.[18]

With documentaries like *The Social Dilemma*, and events like the testimony of former Facebook data scientist Frances Haugen to Congress, many more people are aware of the high risk of everyday algorithmic systems.

With documentaries like *The Social Dilemma* and events like the testimony of former Facebook data scientist Frances Haugen to Congress in October 2021, many more people are aware of the high risk of everyday algorithmic systems.[19] Engagement-based ranking, for instance, is one of the core features of social media sites like Meta (formerly Facebook) and TikTok. The sites show people content based on AI-driven analysis of their past online behavior. The illusion of control is heavily in play. The constant flow of new user-created content, personalized to your habits to capture your attention, makes you feel like you're running the system. Meanwhile, the system is actually running you. Its easiest choices prompt you to stay, to see more ads, and to see ads in a context more conducive to supporting them, no matter how harmful the result.[20]

Haugen testified that Meta's Instagram app was leading teenagers to self-hate and self-harm. There were other abuses: for instance, the subtle promotion of hate speech toward ethnic groups. She substantiated her testimony with internal documents, showing that the company's leaders knew all this and approved it. One internal Meta study found that 13.5 percent of teen girls surveyed said Instagram makes thoughts of suicide worse, and 17 percent said it makes eating disorders worse.[21]

Later, sitting down with CBS's *60 Minutes*, Haugen explained that her former employer had spent years promoting profits over safety. "Facebook has realized that if they change the algorithm to be safer, people will spend less time on the site. They'll click on less ads, they'll make less money."[22] She has consistently argued that legislation was needed to force Meta to improve its own platforms. They will not police themselves.[23]

A Risk Thinking Framework

At this moment, a consensus is growing that overarching regulation of AI is needed. It's still not clear what that regulation will cover or how broad its effect will be. There are manifestos like the White House's AI Bill of Rights in the United States and local legislation, like New York's so-called "AI Bias Law," which went into effect in early 2023. This law is intended to prohibit the use of AI systems for hiring decisions unless they are audited for race and gender bias. [24]

> *"As algorithms and other automated decision systems take on increasingly prominent roles in our lives, we have a responsibility to ensure that they are adequately assessed for biases that may disadvantage minority or marginalized communities."*

> —US Senator Corey Booker

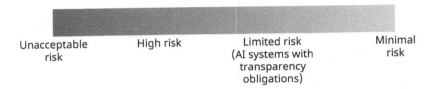

Unacceptable risk · High risk · Limited risk (AI systems with transparency obligations) · Minimal risk

FIGURE 2 A Risk Thinking Framework
Source: Kleiner Powell International (KPI).

"As algorithms and other automated decision systems take on increasingly prominent roles in our lives, we have a responsibility to ensure that they are adequately assessed for biases that may disadvantage minority or marginalized communities," said United States Senator Corey Booker while introducing the proposed Algorithmic Accountability Act in 2022.[25]

The most comprehensive major approach so far is the European Union's Artificial Intelligence Act (AIA). Its proposals have sparked debate about risks and trade-offs, with responses from all four logics of power: the engineering, social justice, corporate, and government perspectives. The Act itself is broad enough and early enough that it will probably set the standard for AI regulation worldwide—if it is ratified.[26]

One major aspect of the proposed law is known as the *pyramid of criticality*.[27] It is a framework for breaking down all Triple-A–related activity—autonomous systems, analytic systems, and AI—into four generally accepted categories of risk, shown in figure 2.[28]

1. Minimal-risk applications do not require oversight because they don't harm people. According to the AIA's proposed framework, AI-enabled video games for children and spam filters fall into this category.

2. Limited-risk apps are those with transparency obligations. For example, chatbots are permitted only if their nonhuman nature is disclosed.

3. High-risk apps include systems that could cause harm to peoples' health, safety, or fundamental rights but also provide significant value to people and society. This category includes self-driving vehicles, credit check systems, and child protection apps designed to tell when children are being abused by their families. When used in a well-considered way, they are valuable; otherwise, they are abusive. In the current draft, the EU would conduct audits, typically with a third-party audit firm or consumer protection nonprofit. To allow for higher levels of innovation, the EU would establish "regulatory sandboxes" where approved projects would be encouraged to experiment without the ordinary audits.

4. Unacceptable-risk apps would be prohibited. These app categories might include real-time biometric identification systems, including many uses by law enforcement; subliminal techniques intended to distort peoples' behavior; apps that exploit the vulnerabilities of particular groups, such as toys that lead children to dangerous behavior; and social-scoring AI systems that favor some people with opportunities while relegating others to outcast status. [29]

If it isn't clear why the EU is planning to severely restrict or ban some uses of AI, consider this comment from Ryan Carrier, founder of the nonprofit ForHumanity, which supports and coordinates independent audits of AI systems: "Some risks sound like science fiction scenarios, but they're all plausible within a few years. With my DNA, you could clone me. Or design a targeted assassination weapon that would only harm me. You could prey on me, based on my psychological or physical profile, or my word choices and emotional responses."[30]

The framework reflects the government logic—and perhaps a sense that others agree. There appears to be a growing perspective that people are losing control of the technology and that only the law can reclaim it. On the other hand, the criteria are vague enough to lead to arbitrary results. "These lists are not justified by externally reviewable criteria," writes legal scholar Lilian Edwards, a professor of law, innovation, and society at Newcastle University. "If it is uncertain why certain systems are on the . . . 'high-risk' lists now, it will be difficult-to-impossible to argue that new systems should be added in the future."[31]

The debates over the AIA are also moving into the realm of digital sovereignty: how much control should a country maintain over the Triple-A systems used within its boundaries or by its people? The current draft states that any company wanting to do business in the EU would have to abandon harmful practices elsewhere as well, including practices by its subcontractors. For example, the company might have to stop selling monitoring and tracking analytics to authoritarian regimes—especially if those regimes used the technology to marginalize some of their own ethnic groups or influence elections in other countries. The AIA's stated rationale for this is that international machine learning could include data output from European algorithmic systems. [32]

The new EU rules, even in draft form, show how important trust will become in preventing risk.

The new EU rules, even in draft form, show how important trust will become in preventing risk. Under these rules, the burden of proof would be on businesses and governments to show that their applications are benign—in intent and in outcomes. In their current form, these new rules mean that companies would publicly articulate the purposes of their technology to ensure that it is trustworthy. Unless there is a clear way to explore the workings of any given Triple-A offering, EU regulators might ban, fine, or restrict its use. Explainability is its own issue, however. We cover it in the next chapter: Open the Closed Box.

CHAPTER 3

Open the Closed Box

You should know when an automated system is being used and understand how and why it contributes to outcomes that impact you.

—Blueprint for an AI Bill of Rights

On the morning of October 28, 2018, a Boeing 737 MAX aircraft nose-dived into the Java Sea just after taking off from Jakarta, killing 189 passengers and crew. Six months later, on March 10, 2019, another Boeing 737 MAX crashed into a meadow shortly after leaving Addis Ababa. On both planes—the first flown by Indonesian airline Lion Air, the second by Ethiopian Airlines—everyone died, a total of 346 people.

After the second crash, US President Donald Trump immediately grounded all MAX 737 aircrafts. Two years of investigations in Indonesia and Ethiopia followed, as well as in the United States, where Congress found Boeing to be responsible. The company lost $20 billion directly—in fines, compensation to the families, and legal expenses—and another $60 billion in abandoned sales. Boeing's CEO Dennis Muilenburg resigned after trying repeatedly to defend the plane and the company. The firm's reputation has been significantly damaged.[1]

A big part of the problem had to do with hiding information, deliberately keeping people from finding out the details related to the automated software in the plane. Muilenburg's defense was a good example. At first, he said there were no technical problems with the plane; then, as the facts emerged, he gave incomplete or misleading answers. This was just one part of a system of "closed boxes," all involving information that wasn't fully disclosed:

1. **An ambiguous aircraft model.** The MAX was a fourth-generation version of Boeing's most popular airplane, the 737. Its release was timed to compete with the Airbus A320neo, and Boeing did not promote it as a major new product, apparently to streamline the release process. Flying the MAX was supposed to be no different from flying previous 737s.

2. **An unacknowledged software upgrade.** The direct cause of the crashes was the code inside the new flight controller, the Maneuvering Characteristics Augmentation System (MCAS). This was an automated system that pushed the nose down when "angle of attack" (AoA) sensors on the plane's fuselage indicated that its trajectory was too high. The company kept the existence of MCAS secret, even after the first crash. "We try not to overload the crews with information," the company explained at a meeting with pilot union representatives.

3. **Too little and too much documentation.** There were two AoA sensors installed on the plane, but only one was connected. Few people knew this, and it wasn't mentioned in the plane's manual.

A pilot safety warning system with alarms was installed in the cockpit, alerting pilots to malfunctions. Here, there was too much information: a confusing array of alerts, different for each 737 model, so that pilots literally had to look up what they meant while trying to land the plane.

4. **Inadequate pilot training.** Because the 737 MAX was an upgrade, there was no flight simulator training for it and only a 56-minute online course—which did not mention the MCAS. Boeing improved the documentation after the first crash, but it still failed to mention the MCAS. The company told the *Wall Street Journal* that it didn't want to overwhelm pilots with information.

5. **Organizational secrecy.** The organizations involved— Boeing, the US Federal Aviation Administration (FAA), and the airlines that had bought the planes—all overlooked warnings in order to get the plane design in the air rapidly at minimal cost. Internal whistleblowers warned that MCAS could lead to crashes, and they were ignored.

There was even an MCAS malfunction in the Ethiopian plane two days before the crash. However, the pilots maneuvered safely through it, and their notes didn't fully document what had happened or provoke alarm.

Why did the company make these choices in secret? Perhaps it had to do with Boeing's culture, concerns about triggering new regulations, embedded internal procedures, or shareholder and competitive pressures. Whatever the specifics, corporate logic prevailed. Again and again, decision makers opted for the most expedient, streamlined options, which generally meant hiding or downplaying anything that might delay the plane's return to the skies. Even after the congressional investigation started, much of the debate had to do with making the plane safe without having to relaunch the whole project.

Ultimately, Boeing did have to recall and then relaunch the MAX. Many of us fly on these planes again, trusting that the company has solved the problem. The plane has been flown since 2020 without mishap. However, all of the damage—to passengers, the company's reputation, and its share price—might have been avoided if Boeing had been more open about its technology and the training needed to master it.

Inside the Closed Box

The term *closed box* is increasingly used to describe Triple-A systems that are unavailable for scrutiny.[2] It is replacing the term *black box*, which also refers to the flight recorder that gathers data for reconstructing events after an airplane accident—a completely different meaning.

The alternative to the closed box is explainable AI—also known as transparent or "open source" AI. These open systems keep the logic and purpose of the software accessible to stakeholders affected by it, so they can question and critique it when necessary. When the inner workings of an algorithmic system are visible to outsiders, it elicits trust in the software system and the company.

> *"Your deep learning model may not be explainable, but you can make it transparent to everyone or select groups, to verify it and reproduce the results. That's how you develop trust."*

—Anand Rao

"Your deep learning model may not be explainable," says Anand Rao, global artificial intelligence lead at PwC, "but you can make it transparent to everyone or select groups, to verify it and reproduce the results. That's how you develop trust."[3]

The most likely reason for closed-box systems is what sociologist and Columbia University professor Diane Vaughan calls "structural secrecy": the innate tendency of government and business to keep their activities hidden from view, even when there are benefits in revealing them. According to Vaughan, the ongoing practice of segregating knowledge can become habitual. If fewer people can make informed decisions, then this reduces the organization's ability to detect and deflect problems. For instance, only a few people knew about Boeing's 737 missteps. The rest of the company could not help if they did not know what was happening.[4]

Structural secrecy and its closed-box systems naturally affect the internal investigative and disclosure practices that companies put in place to manage reputational fallout. University of Virginia law professor Kimberly Krawiec, who conducted an in-depth review in the early 2000s, concluded that most of these investigations are "cosmetic compliance," designed to obscure the details rather than reveal what happened.[5]

Some of us are introduced to structural secrecy as employees. We discover that there's a system in the company that we don't understand—perhaps one that is tracking our own movements or assigning promotions or rewards based on data gathered about us. We aren't sure whether to question it. Some may be cut off from a social media site or be denied access to credit based on corporate policies we don't understand. We might have had a feeling of being in control before, but now it's clear how little real control we have. The closed-box nature of the organizational system is a major reason why.

A Cog in the Dilemma

If your movements were being tracked at work and you wanted to keep your job, would you avoid taking bathroom breaks? Now imagine you were being penalized and your only clue was that your manager asked you why you spent so much time in the bathroom. That's the situation that Amazon workers faced at the company's Staten Island warehouse in 2022. Amazon tracked its packages and workers using the same radio-frequency handheld scanners. That data was integrated into an automated system that calibrated worker movements against the company's expectations using a metric called *time off task* (TOT), and managers were pressured to reprimand workers who slacked off compared to others. This information might never have come to light if it weren't for a labor dispute at a recently-unionized Amazon warehouse in Staten Island, which led to documents being filed with the National Labor Relations Board.[6]

The warehouse workers were also unknowingly forced to compete against one another. On every shift, the employee with the highest TOT score was labeled a "top offender" by the system. Even if everyone performed impeccably by Amazon's standards, there was always at least one person reprimanded by a supervisor. Because the tracking records were concealed, no one knew how much TOT they were racking up. Some refused water and bathroom breaks just to avoid possible TOT. Though Amazon is the second largest employer in the United States as of 2022 and its productivity policies affect hundreds of thousands of workers, it does not openly reveal the algorithms or data policies underlying the TOT tool—not even to employees.

Nor is Amazon the only culprit. A *New York Times* report in August 2022 documented at least a dozen other companies with similar practices, including UnitedHealthcare, JPMorgan Chase,

Barclays Bank, the Kroger supermarket chain, and many others. The monitoring software was often incorrect. People were tagged as idle when away from their desks talking about work problems. Though some companies allowed people to question the outcomes, it was generally discouraged. The stress of structural secrecy led a number of people to quit.[7]

Many of these tracking algorithms reflect the tech industry's liking for secrecy. When we met up with AI systems executive Casey Cerretani in New York in the summer of 2019, he was matter-of-fact about it. He sees the same dynamic job after job in Big Tech. He will be hired to drive a major software project designed to solve a complex problem. The coding job is broken down into more than 100 microtasks, with a team assigned to each, and projects are given names like "Maven" or "Dragonfly" that deliberately hide their nature. Staff members receive information on a strict need-to-know basis, depending on their silos. There is no single "source of truth" that gives everyone a sense of the whole system.

Inevitably, says Cerretani, concerns about ethics surface. "But no individual coder can raise a compelling warning flag," he says, "because very few people understand how the algorithms fit together or what they can do. And each of those slices of the pie are so small. There's a handful of people that see this larger context."

Those who see the larger context are often discouraged from acting on it. "At one company," Cerretani recalled, "there were some dissenting engineers attempting to course-correct within their organizational roles. When that proved unsuccessful, they tried again, and again. It became a volatile situation, and it put the company in a position where it had to put in rules that said nobody could ask too many questions. That left people feeling disillusioned."[8]

Why do companies persist in structural secrecy, even at the expense of their high-value tech employees? The habit of structural secrecy is difficult to break. There is also a deliberate disengagement factor. Business leaders want to "behave harmfully and still maintain a positive self-regard and live in peace with themselves," writes psychologist Albert Bandura. "They do so by disengaging moral self-sanctions from their harmful practices. These psychosocial mechanisms of moral disengagement operate at both the individual and social system levels."[9]

The opacity of these systems is directly linked to the harm they do. Cathy O'Neil, author of *Weapons of Math Destruction*, has built a career around tracing that harm. "[Algorithmic] verdicts land like dictates from the algorithmic gods," she wrote. "The model itself is a black box, its contents a fiercely guarded corporate secret.... [AI systems] are, by design, inscrutable black boxes. This makes it extra hard to definitively answer the question: Does the model work against the subject's interest? Is it unfair? Does it damage or destroy lives?"[10]

Explainability is a prerequisite for trust. If the system can't tell you why it made the decision in the first place, how can you ever hope to push back against it and say, Hey, I'm innocent? Without that ability, if you get sentenced by an algorithm, you can't push back. You can't trust a system that you can't challenge with confidence. Explainable systems are a matter of human dignity, of having a voice in the kinds of decisions that are being made about us.

The XAI Way

Explainable AI (XAI) draws on a long tradition of explainable software. The open-source movement has been active since the 1960s. Unix, Linux, and Netscape Navigator were influential examples of the open-source concept, which was formalized in

1998 with the founding of the Open Source Initiative. Under this model, source code is not just published but made available for comment, adaptation, and uses that were not originally anticipated. It allows software development to build on the talents, contributions, and critique of millions of programmers. Wikipedia and Quora exist in part because of their open-source ethics.[11]

A team of researchers from the Defense Advanced Research Projects Agency (DARPA) studied the concept of XAI between 2015 and 2020. They interviewed or observed more than 12,700 XAI users. They found that when the projects created explanations that people understood, the "additional supervision" of having more observers and questioners tended to correlate with more accurate representations of the world.[12]

The purpose of XAI is not to have explainability for the sake of explainability; rather, it is to help people assess whether the system is reliable. Nontechnical people in particular need to know if the guidance from a Triple-A system makes sense. They need knowledge about its provenance and its assumptions to challenge it meaningfully.[13]

A truly explainable system is open to different levels of explainability: one for technical people, one for the C-suite, one for auditors, one for lawyers, one for regulators, and one for the public. Stakeholders may overlap, but each group needs its own type of explanation because different people understand complex technologies in different ways.

Secrecy in Plain Sight

When an algorithm scours millions of images to learn to recognize a cat, it can still only identify a cat about 85 percent of the time. In contrast, by the time children are three, they can recognize a cat 98 percent of the time. They can even identify the cat in Tom and Jerry, an animated series. The child is much more consistent than the algorithm. Moreover, neither the algorithm nor the toddler can explain the logic involved. Neither has a hypothesis about what correlations might appear.

From this perspective, machine learning is like the toddler. No matter how much you ask it to explain itself, it can't. Reasons for outcomes are generally mysterious, even to the teams who write the code and design the system. Many tech companies simply optimize algorithms to extract data to see what emerges and what they can monetize from it. They regard explanations and documentation as a form of "overengineering": the addition of unnecessary frills that don't really have a purpose.

In the context of Triple-A systems, even if the source data accurately reflects the population of interest and is reliable, valid, complete, and chosen without selection bias, the models may still need to be questioned.

> *"People are being rounded up based on algorithmic predictions in which the algorithms were trained to take into account both historic data and a bunch of woefully negative assumptions about minorities."*
>
> **—Tymon Mattoszko**

As Tymon Mattoszko, a systems engineer who has been working in the field for 20 years, puts it:

You have no idea what machine learning processes will output because of the complexity inside the closed box. For example, in predictive policing, the system takes data sets on race, zip code, age, sex, education, and several unknown variables, weighted in some obscured order of worth, which cannot take into account the context of the people that the data is meant to be describing, and uses [it] to ultimately make predictions about them. People are being rounded up based on algorithmic predictions in which the algorithms were trained to take into account both historic data and a bunch of woefully negative assumptions about minorities. But just because you are a Black male teenager living in a poor neighborhood doesn't make you a criminal.[14]

In other words, correlation is not causation.

Documentation and Explainability

In 2016, the DeepMind Challenge Match between Alphabet's AlphaGo and human Go grandmaster Lee Sedol made headlines around the world. AlphaGo moved in a way that surprised Sedol, and the computer won the challenge. Nobody could explain how AlphaGo made its moves, and to try was futile.[15]

Triple-A systems have decidedly nonhuman ways of performing tasks, which, in some cases, work better than what humans might do. For example, these systems may be expert at learning and detecting patterns that get humans stuck in suboptimal solutions, and they may act on this knowledge in a way that humans would not even consider.[16]

Some argue that we shouldn't even try for explainability. "People can't explain how [AI systems] work, for most of the things they do," says Geoff Hinton, a cognitive psychologist and computer scientist at the University of Toronto and Google. "If you ask them to explain their decision, you are forcing them to make up a story. Neural nets have a similar problem." Therefore, he argues, software should be solely judged on its outcomes; if it is shown to do harm, stop. Having lawmakers and regulators seek documentation for AI systems "would be a complete disaster."[17]

On the other hand, without clear documentation, it is often difficult to prove that the system has done harm. For example, credit bureaus may favor one neighborhood over others in assigning credit scores, or a court may refuse parole based on a predictive algorithm. You can infer from those outcomes that the software system is negatively biased toward some groups or deliberately harmful. But you still can't say definitively that the software was responsible or prevent the same thing from happening next time by fixing a flaw in the code.

The drive for responsible AI has intensified the call for more viable comments in source code so that stakeholders can trace the logic of the algorithm and the business logic underlying it. But that still doesn't clarify what assumptions were made in the process.

The Best Conclusion, Not the Right Conclusion

At the beginning of our interview with serial tech-preneur David Bankston from his home in Naples, Florida, he turns to his laptop and types "black man" into the search bar. He has done this before. He already suspects what the first result after the ads will say. Sure enough, it's a link to an article about a study from Stanford Law School asserting that if women of color want to be successful, they should marry Caucasian men.[18] If you were to click through to the article and read it, you would see its true purpose: to score points against prominent politicians who have done this.

One early reviewer of *The AI Dilemma* read the paragraph above and typed in the same words to see what results he would get. Unsurprisingly, he got a different top link—most likely because he is Caucasian.

Why would this Stanford paper be featured, let alone included, in the top results sent to David—an African American man himself, whose query doesn't mention marriage, Black women, white men, or politics? His explanation lays to rest any illusion you might have that search engines are values-neutral.

"Simply put," he said, "BERT [Bidirectional Encoder Representations from Transformers, the natural language processing software underlying many search engines] is designed to interpret what you type, in context. Context is critical to reaching the best conclusion. Notice I say the best conclusion, not the right conclusion. The downside to all of these technologies is that they need to be trained first before deploying. BERT is not fully trained yet, and it's taking in all the wrong data to interpret the context correctly."[19]

Very few people share David's level of awareness. As a tech entrepreneur with a degree in computer science, who works with corporate and governmental clients, he is aware of how biased search engines are. Even when searches insult people, deliver ads instead of ideas, or fail to yield results, many of us don't stop to question the quality of our search results. We also tend to dismiss or ignore the implications of BERT's personalization. Results reflect each user's individual profile, based on past searches and other data that the search engine has gathered from hundreds of millions of people. We have no idea how those variables are weighted and normalized across the whole of the data set.

Google's search algorithm, built on top of open-sourced BERT, is a closed box and a major competitive advantage for the company. Moreover, Google keeps changing its search algorithms—more than once a day on average—so that users can't game them. In other words, even though visibility into the BERT algorithm exists, that doesn't provide visibility into search outcomes.[20]

Explainability and Data

The techniques for explainability will continue to evolve. The benefits are becoming apparent to all four of the logics of power. Business leaders get a clearer idea of what they are doing and what they can do. Government regulators understand what they are regulating and why. Engineers and social justice activists have been driving the open-source movement.

Of course, use cases vary. In researching this chapter, we learned about several different approaches for documenting or auditing algorithmic systems. We opted not to catalog them; they are continually changing, the value of any approach varies by situation, and there are better places to learn about them.[21]

It is always important that the people affected adversely by a Triple-A system be able to obtain an understanding of what happened. For example, in the Boeing case, it isn't enough to know about the programming of the MCAS, the gathering of the sensor data, or even the training of the pilots. You have to be able to understand the whole sociotechnical system—why it was set up that way, what risks were involved, and how all that led to the crashes. You have to open the closed box of the whole system.

"AI should always be a teacher," says physicist Marka Szabolcs, "and never an overlord. Mapping explainable systems is insufficient. We need to understand why and how they do what they do."

Reconciling the four logics requires not just access but thoughtfulness: a frame of mind in which you are willing to explore technological, human, and organizational behavior and how they interrelate.

"AI should always be a teacher," says physicist Marka Szabolcs, "and never an overlord. Explainable systems are systems we understand. Mapping them is insufficient. We need to understand why and how they do what they do. A lean and fully understood system inevitably leads to better speed, safety, and less energy waste."[22]

When we talked to Alan Morrison about this, he agreed and recalled his days as a young intelligence analyst in the United States Navy. Morrison is a bespectacled and kindly researcher, analyst, and forecaster focusing on advanced digital technologies. His writing has made him one of the top-ranked contributors to Quora. "I was collecting data about planes," he recalls. "We would be very systematic about the whole data life cycle and every format in the collection environment: imagery, voice traffic emissions, electronic emissions, and any aspect of human intelligence. People in a central office put all this together for analysis. There were transcription and archiving systems." Through that meticulous effort, he says, they gained a deep understanding of the data, its provenance, and the potential risks.

More recently, he has worked with multinationals and says he misses the deliberate approach that he learned in the Navy. "I don't see us collecting the right data inside businesses. We're not managing according to the data life cycle. We're not using scalable methods like knowledge graphs to help us. Business-people do some small things to track data, but the big picture is escaping most."[23]

In the next chapter, we will see how Triple-A systems collect data, what they do with it, and how it affects us when it is analyzed and monetized. If you owned your personal data, how would it affect your relationship to it and to those around you?

CHAPTER 4

Reclaim Data Rights
for People

You should be protected from abusive data practices via built-in protections, and you should have agency over how data about you is used.

—Blueprint for an AI Bill of Rights

Talent is randomly distributed across society, but opportunity is not. Data can be used as an alternative way to qualify people for jobs, replacing the biases that underlie many hiring decisions.[1] When the Covid-19 pandemic started, Catherine Booker was looking for a job. She had graduated from college in 2019 with a degree in intercultural communications and Spanish. She wanted an engaging and fulfilling career, and she thought she might learn to code. There was only one problem: as a young woman of color who had never taken a computer science or engineering course, Booker didn't fit the profile of people who software teams typically hire.

Data can be used as an alternative way to qualify people for jobs, replacing the biases that underlie many hiring decisions.

She saw an ad from a Baltimore-based company called Catalyte with an unusual offer. They would train her to code for free if she passed their online test. The test contained puzzles and calculations, like the math part of a Scholastic Aptitude Test [SAT]. It didn't just collect her answers—it monitored how she answered: her speed and the order of her movements. In other words, it was collecting a key component of her personal data: her online behaviors, aptitudes, and areas of interest. Instead of using this data to categorize her or sell to her, Catalyte was using it with her awareness and full cooperation, to help her get employed.

The SAT-style tests showed that she did indeed have the combination of acumen and interest that indicate innate programming skills. That qualified her to join Catalyte's half-year-long immersive "boot camp" training program, where she learned to code in Python and other languages. After she finished, she interviewed with Bloomberg, which was a Catalyte client, and began a one-year contract with them. They ultimately hired her in a career-track position. Without this use of her data, she would never have known about the job, and she might not have discovered her affinity for it.[2]

Catalyte hires and trains coders from a wide variety of backgrounds—including from the liberal arts like Booker, and many people from underinvested communities. On average, these recruits produce code faster with fewer errors than graduates of traditional university computer science programs.

Another firm, Arena, places people in clinical, administrative, and managerial roles for healthcare providers. It uses their behavioral and other personal data, analyzed with machine learning, to identify where they will fit well. Turnover was a major problem in healthcare even before Covid-19. The turnover rates for Arena recruits are much lower on average than people who come in through ordinary recruiting processes. Its machine learning system is deployed into healthcare providers whose applicants represent about 3.7 million unique applicants per year, or about 17 percent of the US healthcare workforce.[3]

In financial services and mainstream business, a nonprofit called Opportunity@Work uses data to successfully place people without college degrees in "gateway jobs," such as customer service representatives or first-line supervisors. These jobs lead to higher-paid professional positions such as bank loan officers or operations managers.[4] In education, a start-up called Amira Learning collects data by asking children aged 5 to 10 to read aloud and assigns them targeted AI-based tutoring.[5]

In all these use cases, personal data is the key element in bypassing the various biases of conventional recruiting. It turns out that for many jobs, formal education is not the best predictor of success.

Many of us are aware that personal data can be aggregated to constrain or take advantage of us. The reality of using it to help people by qualifying them—and thus bypass conventional ways of qualifying people—is harder to accept. For example, many of Catalyte's clients do not acknowledge publicly that they have star software employees who came in without computer science degrees.

The first such client to speak out publicly was Nike. In 2011, Nike hired a team of Catalyte software engineers for its Fuelband wearable. The team stepped in at the eleventh hour, delivered on time, and aced the demo at the product launch.

The director of Nike's digital platform took them all out for drinks to celebrate. She asked where they had worked before, expecting them to name tech companies. The first coder had worked at Taco Bell. The second at a gas station. The third had held odd jobs, like raising dogs to chase geese. The fourth, who had a degree in theoretical physics from China, hadn't been able to land a position in the United States at all. Yet they had all succeeded on a project where Nike engineers had failed. From that point forward, Nike was much more prone to work with people who had been verified with similar data-driven approaches.[6]

The point of this story is not about Nike, Catalyte, or any particular company—or even about recruiting. It is about the use of personal data. In these cases, personal data is used for investment in people: in improving their lives and situation. While the algorithms are typically kept confidential, everyone knows what data has been collected about them. People like Catherine Booker can raise questions if they feel they have been misrepresented by their behavioral data, and groups like Catalyte will recalibrate accordingly. These recruiting systems, to some extent at least, have reclaimed data rights for people.

Privacy Not Included

Now consider how most companies collect and use personal data. By personal data, we mean information that can lead to the identification of a person like you, or can provide sensitive information about you to others. Depending on the jurisdiction, personal data includes names, identification numbers, locations, and physical, physiological, genetic, mental, economic, cultural, and social attributes of the person. Information about us captured through audio or video recording, including security cameras and surveillance devices, are also included in the definition. Even the biometric data that unlocks our phones and authenticates our identity is part of the personal data mix.[7]

It is important to note that even anonymized personal data, stripped of names and ID numbers, can be used to link back to us. Researchers from the University of Texas identified individual people by name from an anonymous database of Netflix movie ratings.[8] This reidentification can happen with as little as two data sets: in this case, movie-watching history and an IMDb database of reviews. The combination of personal details that give data analytics its predictive power also makes it intrusive. Two or more random data points, even if data sets are "sanitized"—stripped of direct identifiers—can be combined to identify any one of us.

We are all vulnerable to the exploitation of our personal information. We are what we reveal.

We are all vulnerable to the exploitation of our personal information. *We are what we reveal.* If someone has never met you, your online presence based on your personal data makes the first impression.

That's one major reason Triple-A systems tend to lead to a loss of real control over your data trails. We cannot control the personal data that organizations collect about us. Nor can we control what happens to it or how it is used. One place where organizations can start building trust is by building transparency in the collection and use of training data. Knowing and trusting a data set can lead to trusting the system trained on it. Vulnerable populations lack trust, and with good reason, since training data has been uneven and not diverse enough to represent the populations of interest.

Behavioral Surplus

Journalist and entrepreneur John Battelle has long been interested in the risks associated with personal data. In 2019, he and a team of data scientists at Columbia University's School of International and Public Affairs analyzed the data-harvesting practices of several Big Tech companies. They developed data visualizations to show the range and density of activity and discovered a few surprises. "In our research we found that Apple collected, or had access to collect, as much if not more data as Google and Facebook," Battelle told us.[9]

The terms of service of most popular apps and devices offer little protection. In a report titled "Privacy Not Included," the Mozilla Foundation behind Firefox has publicly evaluated these agreements since 2017 to see how personal information is treated. The protections for users' data simply aren't there.

For example, Mozilla found that the apps people turn to for counseling are what project lead Jen Caltrider called "exceptionally creepy. They track, share, and capitalize on users' most intimate personal thoughts and feelings, like moods, mental state, and biometric data."[10]

The same is true for prayer apps that record people's prayers. More recently, the Mozilla Foundation's report evaluated apps that women use to track ovulation cycles. These apps have similarly poor scores for guaranteeing that the data won't be shared with, for example, law enforcement or advocate groups.

Mozilla ended up sending queries to 18 of the 25 mental health, prayer, and women's health apps that the project evaluated. The queries asked about their data misuse. Only a small percentage of the app producers responded.[11] They are, of course, only a tiny fraction of the apps gathering data all the time.

Much of this type of data is what Shoshana Zuboff calls "behavioral surplus."[12] It captures more than just purchasing records or online activity. It reveals intimate details about location, age, profession, lifestyle choices, past travel, health, credit scores, habits, and preferences. This granular data is used as fuel for predictive algorithms. It can be monetized to create targeted advertising with predictive capabilities. It may also be used in more problematic ways.

This Is Not a Game

At the 2022 Winter Olympic Games in Beijing, all visitors, athletes, dignitaries, and press were required to download a government-sanctioned app on their phones or else they could not enter.[13] The app, called My2022, was officially mandated as part of the country's protection against the Covid-19 virus. However, the app went far beyond vaccination verification, contact tracing, or social distancing. It automatically recorded and retained all of the user's contacts, social media posts, emails, Internet browsing, and other personal information. As a result, Bloomberg reported that other countries' governments told the athletes and team staff to leave their phones at home and to use a burner phone instead, to dodge spying.[14]

New cases of systematic personal data misuse continue to emerge into public view, many involving covert use of facial recognition. In December 2022, *MIT Technology Review* published accounts of a long-standing iRobot practice. Roomba household robots record images and videos taken in volunteer beta-testers' homes, which inevitably means gathering intimate personal and family-related images. These are shared, without testers' awareness, with groups outside the country. In at least one case, an image of an individual on a toilet was posted on Facebook.[15] Meanwhile, in Iran, authorities have begun using data from facial recognition systems to track and arrest women who are not wearing hijabs.[16]

There's no need to belabor these stories further. There are so many of them. It is important, however, to identify the cumulative effect of living this way. We lose our sense of having control over our lives when we feel that our private information might be used against us, at any time, without warning.

At the same time, many of us treat our personal data as if it has little value. We agree to online terms of service without reading them. We know that personal data is extremely valuable. Companies spend a lot of money gathering it, aggregating it—and protecting their rights to it. Yet it's too time-consuming and confusing to protect our own. We need to change the dynamic. The legal agreements and fine print give us the illusion of control. Let's explore what can be done to gain genuine control.

A Crash Course Called #WeTheData

In 2012, Juliette cofounded, along with 50 data scientists and Intel Labs, a project that illuminated how personal data is used and abused. She also received a crash course on the benefit of sharing personal data to solve the world's greatest challenges. At the time, she was a TED mentor, working with others in the TED community. Intel Labs asked TED fellow and ecologist Eric L. Berlow to map the global ecosystem of personal data. He then invited

Juliette, data artist David Gurman, and branding expert Emily Aiken to help answer the research question: What kind of personal data is collected around the world, and how is it used?

A few years earlier, Intel had launched its "Data Economy Initiative," a multiyear study with the goal of finding ways for people to benefit more completely from the use of their personal data. For instance, if individuals' health data, shopping habits, and behavior online could be tracked and analyzed together over time, this might provide insights around the economics of climate change mitigation or help prevent a pandemic. What would it take to set up systems that would allow personal data to be used in such beneficial ways?[17]

Juliette had already come to understand the link between personal data and identity, and at her suggestion the project, originally called the "Vibrant Data Project," was renamed WeTheData. They sought out experts in related fields—computer scientists, data scientists, anthropologists, investors, and software experts, including Internet legends John Battelle and Kleiner Perkins partner Bill Joy. They filmed interviews with the experts, asking for their observations about the data ecosystem. Amelia Rose Barlow—who worked on the project as a producer—invited her father, John Perry Barlow of the Electronic Frontier Foundation (EFF), to participate. "[The EFF] spends a lot of time trying to get organizations not to retain data that isn't necessary for assuring identity and maintaining convenience of transaction, but that's getting to be very difficult to do," he said in his interview. "I think what everybody wants is sufficient control over their personal data so they don't feel compromised, so their identity is not easy to steal, and they're not a target for endless marketing."[18]

The WeTheData team brought these same people together in a conference and again in workshops to discuss their ideas in detail. They mapped the relationship between their insights and then consolidated them into key points. Two of these key points stand out for us.

First, anonymization was important. If personal data was captured, the identity of each individual could be revealed. This was problematic, especially in countries whose citizens were under constant surveillance.

Second, the use of personal data was monetized by the companies that collected it or by third parties like data brokers. These companies were the only entities that seemed to have control. Everyone else, including the regulators and individuals involved, had no influence over how the data was used, and nobody but the companies that gathered it could access it or earn any money from it. At the time, the most visible benefits of personal data were through companies like Groupon, which pooled similarly minded people to get discounts on purchases. If firms could make money this way, why couldn't we, the people who provided the data in the first place? For instance, why couldn't we direct companies like Groupon, or Facebook and Apple for that matter, to pay a percentage of the money they made from personal data back to users?

Trust, Infrastructure, Access, Literacy

After the research phase ended, the WeTheData team continued the conversation in various ways, asking for peoples' insights and experience. Their work was featured in a discussion on personal data at the World Economic Forum in 2011. Juliette kept leading the community back to the core question: What would it take for people to truly be in control of the data we generate instead of the other way around?[19]

By exploring what would be required for us to take back control of personal data, our research team yielded four key prerequisites or grand challenges. If they weren't nourished in the larger ecosystem simultaneously, then far fewer people in the world would have a real say on how their personal data is used.

The four grand challenges are as follows:

1. **Digital trust.** People need confidence that they will not be betrayed by the use of their devices. For example, if you allow your phone to unlock with facial recognition or fingerprint biometrics, can you trust the companies involved to keep your facial and fingerprint data protected even if there are security breaches?
2. **Digital infrastructure.** In your community, do you have electricity? Do you have the infrastructure for high-bandwidth Internet that is connected to the world and the devices with which to explore online?
3. **Digital access.** If a group is restricted from using the system while another group is not, then there is a disparity in digital access.
4. **Data literacy.** Could you query a data set? Could you question conclusions that you saw in a report by looking at the source data? Can you tell when outcomes are skewed?[20]

WeTheData also found that more than 95 percent of the personal data gathered in the world was—then and now—managed by companies that were monetizing it through advertising and promotion. Some companies, like Facebook with Cambridge Analytica, would sell or give away data for use in political campaigns. A few countries, like Finland, had systems that allowed people to manage their own data and monetize it through their bank; Finnish and Estonian healthcare systems could also share personal data across their border.[21] Keep in mind these are high-trust societies. Other countries were beginning to collect data and giving people no control over it at all.

Here we are about 10 years later, and the situation hasn't changed. Tech companies are still gathering more data than ever about all aspects of human, machine, and organizational behavior. Companies are still exploring novel ways to use it, with few controls. The largest effort to regulate this data free-for-all, the European Union's General Data Protection Regulation (GDPR), has halted some abuses. It is no longer legal in Europe to spam people with unsolicited emails, and this has become the norm in many other parts of the world. In the United States, the Health Insurance Portability and Accountability Act (HIPAA) has also established guardrails against some misuse.

Nonetheless, the basic asymmetries of power remain. Companies and governments gather personal data. The cost of gathering it is low, and people have little or no say in how it is used or aggregated. The economic value of personal data varies by individual. If you are a middle-class person in a wealthy community, a social media or e-commerce firm might sell your data for about 50 cents. If you are searching for vacation information, getting a divorce, or coping with a health problem that requires medication, your data might be worth more. The data's value depends on how your personal characteristics are ranked. Finally, much of the data about you that is sold is probably out of date. One 2019 estimate suggested that the average Facebook user's data was worth $2/month to the company. It might have changed since then. The Financial Times data value calculator, still active today, was published back in 2013.[22]

Penny for Your Data?

Many people will be talking about data privacy over the next few years. The core issue enabling the right to privacy is data rights: the ability to control who sees information about you, how it is seen, and how it is used. The European Data Protection Board fined Meta €390 million in January 2023 for not giving its users clear options for regulating the data collected about them, and other cases will probably follow around the world.[23]

Even now, however, it is not clear what data ownership means. One key measure of your level of control is whether you can be paid for the use of your personal data.

Suppose every company that collects personal data about you had to pay you for it. One place where we may see this is with Web3 technology, using blockchain to manage the details. MobileCoin, a cryptocurrency start-up founded by CEO Joshua Goldbard, is set up as this type of privacy-focused payment platform.[24] The idea is to protect user data and computations.

"There are enough systems in place," says AI and cloud solutions architect Sean Gayle, "to monetize personal data back to the individual. You could set it up to tax the largest companies so that they can pay the freight and use the money to address larger issues like climate change."

Gayle also says that the legal and regulatory climate may be shifting to make control of personal data more feasible. "Balancing the marketing outcomes of collecting and using PII [personally identifiable information] with the regulatory, compliance, and governance aspects of collecting, storing, and using an individual's personal data is a slippery slope," he told us. "It has brought many large brands to their knees and resulted in huge payouts as fines for the mishandling, misuse, and even abuse of the data."[25]

Anand Rao, global artificial intelligence lead at PwC, suggests a framework for data rights and payments. This framework is based on the concept of fractional ownership—of using blockchain to make the interchange of data rights relatively seamless, backed up by government regulation. He proposes a group of data banks, established to monitor who gets to use data, for what purpose, and for what duration.

"I should be able to tell an insurance company that they can analyze my health record," he suggests. "They can use it to quote me a life insurance policy. But I don't want them to keep a record, and they must delete it after one week."

> *"Pick a vector. Climate change, human trafficking, you could pick any of these atrocious situations that we're facing as a global community and then identify and hold accountable companies that are directly or indirectly aiding and abetting some of those. From there, you do not sell software to them. Ever."*
>
> —Casey Cerretani

Casey Cerretani—the executive with experience developing software, hardware, and consumer products in small and large enterprises and nonprofits—also agrees that people should be paid for their personal data when it is monetized. Moreover, he sees a world in which we would also use aggregated data from society and the predictive power of Triple-A systems to benefit the world, not just to sell more products and services. "Pick a vector. Climate change, human trafficking, you could pick any of these atrocious situations that we're facing as a global community and then identify and hold accountable companies that are directly or indirectly aiding and abetting some of those. From there, you do not sell software to them. Ever."[26]

Perhaps in the future we will each have a trusted personal AI that looks out for us by mediating these relationships behind the scenes. Questions about the value of data might fall to these data banks or to these personal AI systems; they may keep track of how much companies are paying for different data packages that your data is involved in. As tech innovator Jaron Lanier, economist E. Glen Weyl and others have proposed, the role of data provenance could be handled by "mediators of individual data," volunteer organizations similar to labor unions. Lanier and Weyl estimate that some individuals could earn $20,000 from their data per year.[27] Government agencies could oversee the process, as they oversee banks today. "Money is important enough to be regulated," Rao says. "Why shouldn't data be the same?"[28]

If you could monetize your data somehow, what would you expect to earn per year? In her research at Columbia University, Juliette asked this question of hundreds of people in the United States and Finland. The most common reply was that the annual amount should roughly equal what they spent playing online games and on their subscriptions to online media like Netflix, Amazon Prime, and Apple TV.[29]

In chapter 5, Confront and Question Bias, we will explore why companies and sometimes governments, even when they espouse egalitarian values, consistently put biased processes in place.

CHAPTER 5

Confront and Question Bias

You should not face discrimination by algorithms, and systems should be used and designed in an equitable way.

—Blueprint for an AI Bill of Rights

Solutions architect Sean Gayle is one of the inventors of the EZ-Pass. His machine learning skills are self-taught; his degree from a historically Black college is in psychology. He says, "The problem with bias in machine learning is GIGO: garbage in, garbage out. For example, I worked with one large company that used machine learning to determine people's ages from their faces. Invariably for the Black faces, they got the ages completely wrong—by decades. The problem started with the hundreds of thousands of images that were entered into the system as input. They were white corporate people, from highly educated backgrounds. They didn't have enough examples of people's faces from more diverse backgrounds."

Voice recognition is similarly biased. Gayle uses a different voice for different AI applications. To operate his navigator app in his truck, for example, he uses what he calls his "insurance salesman voice," which is a voice devoid of Black culture or references.

When he gives us an interview, however, he naturally reverts to the voice and expressions he uses with his fraternity brothers. When he uses this voice, the AI-based transcription app we used for this book had a perceptibly lower accuracy rate than it did with his salesman voice or other Caucasian-sounding voices. So did a person we asked to check on the AI's work. She misidentified many of Gayle's expressions.

Gayle explains that most machine language systems have a natural language processing capability that is daisy-chained with voice recognition capability. For the machine to detect the words, or even something as simple as the person's gender, you have to teach these two systems not just about different pitches and sounds but about the social contexts that affect the way people speak.

"Engineers who [train the machines] are not necessarily the most socially adept humans in the world," Gayle explains. "You're asking them to be able to open their minds up to stuff that they don't experience in the real world. So they've baked that limited view of the world into the system they're working with."

Gayle has worked in the field of machine learning for 20 years. "But no matter how I try, I can't fully blend in. I still hear colleagues tell me: 'I'm amazed you know as much as you do. Black people are not predisposed to engineering. Where did you learn that from?' I've heard Black people called 'slick' when they talk fast, and I've heard people who speak with a Southern drawl being called slow, even if they're the smartest people in the room."

He trains himself to speak, he says. "To be successful in IT, I have to make myself very vanilla. I have to be very careful, sui generis, including my tone. I have a mirror in front of my computer so I can see myself smiling. And I always use mouthwash, so my breath is fine. I put on my blended white voice, my insurance salesman voice. If I don't do all this, I find that people do not take me seriously.

"I don't speak out about this," Gayle continues. "But I make corrections in subtle ways. For instance, there's a common server-client connection generally called 'master-slave.' I'll use 'primary-secondary' instead. No one gives it a second thought, and it gradually catches on. I don't correct other people when they say 'master-slave' because I'm not trying to make people feel bad. It's just that the expression doesn't work for me." The burden of confronting and questioning bias tends to fall to individuals. That is not a recipe for success. There are, however, several ways in which the tech community is mobilizing or adapting—not to eliminate bias, per se, but to bring it to a moderate level where the algorithms deserve our trust.[1]

People are biased, so workplaces are biased, and as a result the outcomes of AI systems are biased.

Workplace studies suggest that experiences like these are common.[2] People are biased, so workplaces are biased, and as a result the outcomes of AI systems are biased. In Art's years of observing and working at large companies, he saw many cases of employees who were shut out because they didn't fit in. Most corporate, government, and academic cultures have an ingrained negative bias against people who don't match the established way of speaking and behaving. It's quite possible for them to succeed and thrive but only by "going corporate." Many neurodiverse people or people from underrepresented backgrounds, for example, feel the need to create an assimilated persona that is on the same temperamental and cultural wavelength as those within the company. Those who don't put on the mask are at risk of being othered—not being favored, and not being treated as important.

This reality shapes the bias of automated and algorithmic systems. Through many subtle decisions and placements made during the design of the software and the selection of data, people in the prevailing cultural wavelength are favored. The bias inherent in AI thus adds another weight to the othering that people already feel, as it reflects the culture around them.

Where the Biases Are

Bias in Triple-A systems is an everyday occurrence. Researchers at the Georgetown Law School estimated that 117 million American adults are in facial-recognition networks used by law enforcement—and that African Americans were most likely to be singled out because they were disproportionately represented in mug-shot databases.[3]

Negative biases like these are self-reinforcing. As each new decision builds on the presumed success of previous decisions, the historical weight of bias increases and the negative consequences escalate. The visible effect is to raise the number of false identifications—and thus to raise the likelihood of being targeted: arrested without cause or denied jobs, housing, or opportunities.

In 2018, Joy Buolamwini and Timnit Gebru—computer scientists who then held research posts at the MIT Media Lab and Microsoft, respectively—copublished an influential paper called *Gender Shades*. Buolamwini has a PhD from MIT; her thesis is titled "Facing the Coded Gaze with Evocative Audits and Algorithmic Audits".[4] Gebru has a PhD from Stanford University and did her postdoc at Microsoft. In *Gender Shades,* they assessed three of the most prominent facial-recognition systems that were then available. These systems had been trained with the same two benchmark data sets, IJB-A and Adience, which between them had millions of images. In all three facial recognition systems, the error rates were significantly higher for people of color, especially for women of color. A quarter to a half of the darker-skinned women's faces generated errors. Two of the three systems performed only slightly better than a random guess. By contrast, only 1 percent to 12 percent of the three systems generated errors when working with Caucasian faces, particularly white male faces.[5]

By 2019, Buolamwini had set up the Algorithmic Justice League and worked with Gebru to take their research further. This time, they set up an auditing study of algorithm-based systems that had explicitly included images of people of color in training data sets.

"The algorithms still performed better on lighter-skinned than darker-skinned faces," the researchers wrote. "[They] performed better on male-identified faces than female-identified faces and performed worse on women of color. Even if accuracy disparities are within a few percentage points, differential accuracy on millions or hundreds of millions of people will impact substantial quantities of individuals."[6]

These skewed results prompted action, including testimony before a congressional committee, and added momentum to a growing movement of concern around negative racial bias.

Since then, broad appeals have been made, including one from the Association of Computing Machinery, asking for moratoriums on the use of facial-recognition systems by governments, including criminal justice, military, and child welfare uses, until the discriminatory bias is addressed.[7]

Garbage In, Garbage Out

Algorithms are not biased in themselves. They amplify and solidify the attitudes that are already prevalent in people. The algorithms, models, and training data are selected by people and built around human assumptions. Our negative biases are fed into systems as data: garbage in, garbage out. There is a generalized lack of transparency in a system's training data; knowing and trusting a data set can lead to trusting the system trained on it. Diverse groups lack trust because training data has been uneven and has lacked diversity, "often because of availability and convenience," says entrepreneur Kevin Clark.[8]

> *"It's not the system that's biased. It's the data, and the people involved with the system. People can't help but put their thumb on the scale."*
>
> —**Sean Gayle**

"It's not the system that's biased," says Sean Gayle. It's the data, and the people involved with the system. People can't help but put their thumb on the scale."[9]

Psychologists have identified a number of categories of ingrained bias, and at least three are relevant:

Restraint bias is the tendency to overestimate the level of control we have over our impulsive behaviors. These urges typically come from visceral impulses such as hunger, drug cravings, fatigue, sexual arousal, and yes, you guessed it, our addiction to our digital devices and social media. In any of these examples, we overestimate our control over our mental and physical urges to relax, and we underestimate the influence of fatigue. So we turn to social media, lose track of time, and self-sabotage.

With any addiction, even online addiction, people often demonstrate a strong restraint bias. Their inflated sense of impulse control causes individuals to enter into situations where they are exposed to addictive behaviors because they think their self-control is greater than it is. These behaviors increase the chances of relapse and can cause significant unintended negative outcomes.

Negative bias is the unconscious tendency to accentuate fear and distaste rather than hope and curiosity. It is negative bias that leads us to "other" people: to regard them as dangerous, or underqualified because they are different from us.

In our interview with Cathy O'Neil, which occurred soon after she appeared in *The Social Dilemma,* she pointed out that negative bias is embedded in many machine learning inputs, leading to widespread racism and also to bias against age and people with disabilities. The bias is present in many subtle decisions made by AI system producers, ranging from designing the AI system to selecting the data to justifying and defending the outcomes.[10]

Confirmation bias is the strong tendency to pay more attention to data that reinforces an existing point of view. Algorithms are prone to confirmation bias in the selection of data, the way data is interpreted by the algorithm, and the way the outcomes are used. The iterative function of machine learning can perpetuate the bias and often make it more entrenched.

Triple-A systems can be further biased through the way they are used, which, in turn, may be skewed toward groups of people who found their existing biases confirmed. This helps explain why Triple-A systems are so prone to bias and difficult to correct. "Firms should be wary of positioning AI as the test case when citizens' freedoms are at stake. The forces of tight coupling tend to drive Big Tech, over time, toward misconduct and negative unintended consequences to society," insists AI systems executive Casey Cerretani.[11]

AI thus adds another weight to the othering that people already feel. Joy Buolamwini wrote that she had to wear a white mask for her robot at MIT to recognize her as easily as it recognized white men.[12] Sean Gayle had to change his demeanor and his voice for his virtual assistant to guide him. Lynn Cherny and Casey Cerretani had to quit.

Warming the Data

Institutional sociologist David Stark says that confronting bias requires us to confront "unreflective activity": to raise awareness, in the moment of tech design, of the presence and impact of bias. "Scripts, routines, and classifications of cultural taken-for-granteds worked as analytic tools [in organizations in the past] because they worked as the operative recipes for behavior in the relatively stabilized institutional environments of the mid to latter part of the last century," he says. Today, "taken-for-granteds are likely to be out-of-date.... But [leaders] look for practices to help unlock the grip of habit."[13]

Here's an example of how that can work, in the context of a problem affecting students of color in school districts around the United States. These students tend to be identified, in disproportionate numbers, as needing special education and related services. The number of Black and Latinx students bearing these labels had been 7 to 10 times greater than students from other race/ethnicity backgrounds. One of the factors was the way that students' personal data was gathered, analyzed, and interpreted.

We learned about this from Jennifer Yales. She works in the California state school system, as one of a group of senior directors for the System Improvement Leads project. A large part of her job requires the exploration and analysis of special education data. She is part of a team that helped develop a new online dashboard that enables school districts to better monitor their special ed performance plans.

Yales cites filmmaker and researcher Nora Bateson, who calls this kind of information "cold data": purely quantitative statistics that don't express the underlying relationships and human interactions that matter most. This type of negative bias seems to be locked into the system and is all the more immovable because it is not acknowledged openly.[14]

"It's hard to change this system because it's hard to see," writes Yales. "The guidelines and expectations for special education are long-established and deeply rooted in the professional culture. To address this, we need to better connect with our own beliefs and have conversations about the data as a part of a system and not just a number. We need to 'warm the data' in the way we talk about it."

In warming the data, she doesn't dispute the metrics. Instead, she introduces a wider range of information. "There can be multiple descriptions of a child's situation," she says, "coming from different observers, not just one educational evaluator. The findings can refer to similar patterns of behavior found with other students, who may have ended up placed in different ways. The data can include changes over time, in the relationships with adults or other children, or in the types of behavior. There could be more discussion of the context, including the community, the economics, and other factors."

Yales and other concerned colleagues are thus setting up regular sessions to discuss children's data along with its biases. "Creating a conversational space where we could weave qualitative data along with quantitative data, creates a more complete understanding of each child's context. Stories and interviews with the children and their families show personal realities underlying the statistics."[15]

The stories in this chapter all suggest ways of confronting and questioning bias. They all involve warming the data in some way: bringing the alternative way of looking at things to people's attention. In chapter 6, on holding stakeholders accountable, we will see how this type of confrontation plays out when there are organizational issues at stake.

CHAPTER 6

Hold Stakeholders Accountable

You should be able to opt out, where appropriate, and have access to a person who can quickly consider and remedy problems you encounter.

—Blueprint for an AI Bill of Rights

Just because you can doesn't mean you should," said Peter Sloly, former Chief of Police for the Ottawa Police Service. He was referring to the free trials of Clearview AI's facial recognition software and its use in police work. The technology has been associated with systematic misidentification of darker-skinned people. Moreover, the American Civil Liberties Union (ACLU), the Electronic Frontier Foundation (EFF), and other groups have contested its use on principle because it can be used to single out immigrants, sex workers, and survivors of domestic violence. The police moratorium on the software was voluntary and happened before the Canadian Privacy Commission ruled the software illegal in April 2021.[1] "For practical applications,

Clearview AI was all the rage," said Sloly. "But police chiefs actually held themselves in check and voluntarily put it back on the shelf. The police decided they shouldn't have it, let alone use it."[2]

Stateside, Clearview AI was affected by a series of events that began back in 2008, when Illinois passed the Biometric Information Privacy Act (BIPA), restricting the capture of facial data or other biometric information. That had generated an agreement from Facebook to curb its gathering of data for facial recognition—not just in Illinois, but across the United States. Thanks to BIPA, the ACLU successfully sued Clearview AI in the state of Illinois. In the 2022 settlement, Clearview AI lost the right to sell its facial recognition technology to private organizations nationwide, with few exceptions.[3]

All these examples show what accountability looks like for emerging technologies like Triple-A—algorithmic, autonomous, and automated—systems. Now let's look at what the absence of accountability might look like.

In the 2010s in the Netherlands, a widespread national social services program provided financial and medical support for low-income families with children. Then in 2013, an estimated 26,000 of these families had their benefits suddenly cut.[4] An algorithmic system had identified them as fraud risks. Those who were not born in the Netherlands, who worked more than one job, or who knew others on the list of fraud risks were more likely to be targeted.

The whole operation was mysterious. There were few criminal prosecutions. No list of risk factors was published. However, if you were on the list of accused families, your life could be ruined. Your last five years of tax filings might be audited. There was no obvious way to defend yourself. You might have to immediately pay back thousands of euros you had received legitimately and on which you and your family depended. The consequences were severe, even for people who helped you. Your tax advisers could be called in for questioning and possibly jailed. Worst of all, you could lose custody of your children. More than 1,500 children were taken from their homes and placed in foster care.[5]

The scandal broke into public awareness six years later, when whistleblowers from the Dutch Tax and Customs Administration sent urgent reports about it to Parliament. It wasn't until 2020, more than seven years after the supposed fraud prevention algorithm began operating, that a lawsuit forced the government to compensate more than 9,000 falsely accused parents.[6] The reason for this operation then came out: the Netherlands government Tax and Customs Administration had discovered that a group of Bulgarian immigrants were defrauding their new national childcare benefits fund. The agency had responded by quietly introducing a new algorithmic system designed to predict fraud, and the abuses had spiraled out from there, with no one taking responsibility for them.

"The black box system resulted in a black hole of accountability," wrote Merel Koning of Amnesty International. "The lack of transparency . . . drove the victims of the childcare benefits fraud system into Kafkaesque legal procedures, with no effective remedies open to the parents and caregivers."[7]

As the Dutch newspaper *Trouw* recounted, "Officials feared the consequences of admitting mistakes too freely. Because if the more than 300 parents in the much-discussed case were to be compensated, how many would follow in other cases? . . . At least 8,500 parents, but it was even feared that this could go toward several hundred thousand. The fear of setting a precedent has since blocked a solution for the victims."[8]

Each step of the way, the Dutch government leaders tried to deny or defend their actions. In the end, they were held accountable—but only to a limited extent.

"The government resigned, indeed," said Christine Moser, an academic who was targeted because she worked with one of the accused accountants. "But they did it only weeks before national elections, making the exercise almost meaningless; and, much worse, they were reelected. So, did the resignation make an impact? No. Are the parents compensated? No. Kids back at home? No, which is the real scandal here."[9]

We see similar government accountability issues in the United States, where we live. It might be happening where you live, too. A 2022 report from the Electronic Privacy Information Center found that algorithms were used across 20 city agencies in Washington, DC, with more than a third deployed in policing or criminal justice. The report compared these automated decision-making systems to judges, who are explicitly held accountable for accuracy, fairness, and equity, and who "must explain their decisions in writing so that everyone can understand their reasoning." By contrast, the algorithms "make decisions without much oversight or input, decisions that are difficult to challenge, and decisions that are unfair."[10] In Michigan, an algorithm used to detect unemployment fraud had a 93 percent error rate, resulting in 40,000 false fraud allegations.[11]

Government logic is not the only factor in solving the problem of accountability for Triple-A systems. We need to look at all four logics of power—engineering, social justice, corporate, and government—and bring them together.

Just Because Government Can, Doesn't Mean It Should

"We're turning over a lot of power to an incredibly powerful state," says Peter Sloly, "layered on top with machine learning and all the other aspects that come with it. These are bigger tools that have less time to inevitable failure than any other tool before. We've given outmoded institutions incredible power. Governments aren't in a position to explain their role, explain the tools they use to maintain the role, or prove the efficacy or ethics of those tools. It's almost an impossible scenario."

AI systems can increase the power of government at every level. This raises new questions about the purpose of government itself.

AI systems can increase the power of government at every level. It changes government practices in subtle ways, where the process is hard to see but the outcomes are clearly visible. As Sloly points out, this raises new questions about the purpose of government itself. Traditionally, he says, the government primarily functions as a protecting entity: "A standing army to protect against other countries and a criminal justice system to protect citizens from one another—are the two most common functions of Western-based democracies." How do you merge the idea of lowering risk for citizens with the singular requirements for technology that a government needs to protect its own citizenry? That's where we need some unpacking. From Sloly's perspective, AI gives the government more capabilities in all of these respects.

"We tend to think the solution involves individual agencies or organizations. The truth is, we should be thinking about ecosystems. If you corrupt the sources of data, then all the components that went into the algorithm have been corrupted from the source." He adds that "they will always produce unintended outcomes. Those unintended outcomes will always affect the weakest, most marginalized, most vulnerable elements of society, which are often the most racialized elements. It's impossible to think that the system would operate in any other way."[12]

Governments can promote Triple-A accountability in several ways. First, they must protect their citizens. This means using and regulating AI systems responsibly, as the AIA and the AI Bill of Rights suggest.

Second, they must safeguard against their own dangerous tendencies. In an era of increasingly powerful AI systems, they must be open enough to allow others to hold them accountable when needed.

Third, governments can provide financial incentives for medium- and long-term investment in responsible technology. This can take the form of government contracts, tax credits, or procurement policies that favor businesses with good track records in developing Triple-A applications that are beneficial to the wider population. One example of this is the US Department of Defense research on explainable AI (XAI) that we mentioned in chapter 3.

Fourth, as governments take on the challenge of regulating Triple-A systems, they have to balance all four logics judiciously. Marc Rotenberg, founder of the Center for AI and Digital Policy, an independent nonprofit based in Washington, DC, commented on this in our conversation with him. To Rotenberg, the effectiveness of AI regulation, as with all regulation, depends not just on the way it is written but on the way it is implemented. Enforcement should be meaningful and consistent: "It's not regulation per se that concerns me. It's the fact that regulators put a structure in place and then ignore it. This is the reason, for example, I've been critical over the years of the US Federal Trade Commission. We've actually sued them for not enforcing the settlements we've helped establish."

Asked for examples of effective regulations, Rotenberg mentions product safety and quality. "We take it for granted that the brakes will work on our car and our toaster won't catch fire. That wasn't always the case. It took regulatory oversight to achieve this. We just don't have that ethic around the tech industry, and now we need to develop it."[13]

In all these areas, the burden of proof is now on governments to show that they can manage this level of accountability. The track record so far is mixed, at best. The Roman satirist Juvenal famously asked, "Who will watch the watchers?" It has been difficult since antiquity to hold power to account. Now, it will be even more difficult. Who will watch the watchrobots?

Are Engineers Accountable?

You might think someone with the title of "data scientist," "software engineer," or "systems architect" should be prepared to assume professional accountability, like a lawyer, doctor, architect, or mechanical engineer. Those professionals are liable if they cause harm through their work. However, data scientists aren't scientists, systems architects aren't architects, and software engineers generally haven't been trained or certified as engineers. They are not generally in a position to stand up to their employers or to their clients, and they don't have the same kind of professional associations taking their side.

"Let's say there are 3 million developers in the United States. Most of them have not been exposed to best practices around responsible AI," explains technology researcher and analyst Alan Morrison. "They may not even understand what the best practices are. You can either dictate a set of best practices and try to enforce them somehow, or you can try to really do something at a small scale within a trusted community."[14]

Tech workers see the abuses from within, and many don't talk about them until they feel pressed to do so. They break the wall of silence only when they are financially independent, like Casey Cerretani; or when someone they care about is threatened, like David Bankston (chapter 3) or Sean Gayle (chapter 5); or when their concerns overwhelm their prudence, like Lynn Cherny (chapter 2) or Meredith Whittaker. Whittaker is the chief adviser of the AI Now Institute. She was an AI engineer at Google who led two walkouts totaling more than 20,000 employees during the 2018 Tech Revolt. The goal was to persuade the company not to bid on certain military contracts involving AI. The protesters were mostly managers and coders from the engineering teams, calling out not just the contract but also separate charges of sexual misconduct. Google ultimately agreed not to bid on the contract, but Whittaker ultimately left.[15]

This is the bind in which many people working within companies, especially those with tech, engineering, or specialized skills, find themselves. They are organizational heretics: people who see a reality that counters the official story of the company and who wish to remain loyal to the company without losing their grip on the other reality. Some leave; some silence themselves. Others try to find a "voice," a way of speaking up within the organization that will not backfire on them. It is possible to find this voice, but usually not on one's own, and it takes some skill—or, as we call it, creative friction (see chapter 8).

If we really want to hold software engineers legally accountable for Triple-A outcomes, then it would take a more rigorous form of training, with regular retraining and recertification. Entrepreneur Kevin Clark agrees: "This could be the role of a new team member, or it can be added to the project management system. With systems writing code, the systems architect becomes a key person in defining the use case, the way it will be approached, and the outcomes."[16]

Finally, engineers aren't necessarily on their own. They can set up dialogues about the changes that are needed. With the escalation of the Tech Revolt of 2017–2019, engineers began sharing their discontent among themselves and with higher-ups. Over time, they elicited shared social justice concerns from other engineers and contractors across Big Tech. As concerns mounted, these other activist groups joined engineers and tech workers in protest, shared petitions, and communicated issues to the press through published interviews and op-eds. This led to even more tech workers joining in and more public awareness.[17]

The Effective Social Justice Activist

As we've seen, people who want to curb negative AI outcomes tend to base their arguments on the social justice logic. They support making all AI stakeholders accountable to each other and to broader society, including those who have been marginalized in the past. If we want to get all the relevant voices in the discussions about AI, the voices of social justice need to be considered as important as the other logics.

Doc Searls, a coauthor of *The Cluetrain Manifesto* and an alumnus at Harvard University's Berkman Klein Center for

Internet & Society uses the word "shield" to describe how activists view their work—protecting citizens from sociotechnical intrusion and manipulation.[18]

The shield is meant to protect the shared vital resources of society: social equity, access to opportunity, participation, and rights. AI systems are now so embedded that they are shared vital resources themselves. As Searls puts it, without the shield provided by the logic of social justice, "what can be done will be done"—at least until we see how destructive such an approach can be when it comes to emerging technology.

Searls argues that regulation of sociotechnical systems should happen before disasters occur. Waiting until after disaster is a cultural strategy that makes the dangers of a given technology "really hard for us to see." The Cambridge Analytica and Facebook user privacy congressional hearing was a "wake up call" to engage with policy that would ensure that in future, the values of social justice would prevail over sociotechnical efficiency and corporate inability to self-regulate on behalf of social interests. In Searls' words: "We want to be able to write that regulation or make sure we have a big influence."[19]

Many long-term efforts are now converging into a movement to evaluate and constrain AI systems. The movement includes leaders like Timnit Gebru, Tristan Harris, and Meredith Whittaker, who left Big Tech and started their own foundations. Others, including Cathy O'Neil and Ryan Carrier, offer Triple-A audits as a way to level the playing field. Many social justice activists in this field have been personally affected by AI overreach or know people who have been.

The activist's role so far has been to frame the terms of debate to reflect the needs of society at large, rather than prioritizing technological, military, and economic growth at society's expense. The most effective voices of social justice demonstrate firsthand knowledge of the people, technologies, and cultures that produce and deploy AI systems. They use their knowledge and their ties to other community stakeholders to develop a collaborative context.

For these activists, the people's right to know is paramount. Improving conditions in society is vital to their projects, including those related to Triple-A systems. Their view of responsible AI centers on social inequality—on holding businesses and governments with unprecedented power accountable for the consequences of their decisions.

Holding Corporations Accountable

Systems engineer Casey Cerretani recalls working with Siemens building servers for medical data: a highly-regulated space. According to the law, Siemens was obliged to decommission servers that held private medical data after a specified length of time. But the company faced a dilemma. If it followed this rule, it would risk breaking another rule related to the environmental impact of decommissioning the servers. "[The first] alternative, to let the servers keep running, was certainly less of a headache," says Cerretani. "In some cases it was economically cheaper"—in other words, more profitable.[20]

Instead of having to deal with the regulated disposal of toxic precious metals inherent in the decommissioning process, firms like Siemens often choose to keep servers running instead. Their data silos thus capture and retain sensitive personal data far longer than is permitted by law, breaching patients' right to privacy. The regulatory fines for disobeying rules around precious metals were far less expensive than doing the work of actually decommissioning servers and protecting patients' privacy.

This is an example of how accountability is often treated within the corporate logic. There are conflicting rules and multiple trade-offs. The most expedient profit motive generally supersedes other choices, even when long-term liabilities or penalties are involved. Companies obey the letter of the law, not the intent or spirit of the law. If there is a growing public concern over lack of social responsibility, new organizational roles are created. Enter the era of the "Chief Ethical Officer" and "Chief Quality Officer"—not as signs of active self-regulation, but rather, according to Cerretani, as regulatory window-dressing.

> **If an organization exhibits genuine responsibility, they're not just talking about diversity in terms of DEI programs. They're reflecting it through the composition of their senior leadership, including their board.**

If an organization exhibits genuine responsibility, they're not just talking about diversity in terms of DEI programs. They're reflecting it through the composition of their senior leadership, including their board. If they're not leading by example, with different ways of looking at the world guiding their top decisions, then that's a strong signal that they are not serious about accountability.

Corporations support self-regulation for Triple-A systems. They argue that as investors and owners, they have more at stake than the other logics—and that they can effectively regulate themselves by putting in place established practices, with their own oversight committees to keep them honest.

However, corporate self-regulation has a poor track record—especially for its impact on noncorporate people and vulnerable groups. Business leaders may espouse responsible AI or good environmental, social, and governance practices. However, most existing corporate accountability removes power from everybody else while claiming legitimacy in upholding the social contract.

The concept of responsible AI has been linked to efforts by Big Tech companies and marketing to promote self-governance instead of regulation. "The idea of using ethics is not problematic in itself," notes the Algorithmic Justice League, "but has led to a proliferation of 'AI Principles' with limited means for translating these principles into practice. . . . This is a limited approach from our perspective because it does not create any mandatory requirements or ban certain uses of AI."[21]

One problem with self-regulation is that it is expensive to do it well. It is very difficult to completely monitor Triple-A systems using automated methods; accountability requires human judgment. As we saw with human moderators like Lynn Cherny struggling with online predatory behavior, applying this judgment can place tremendous stress on people.

Other reasons why self-regulation doesn't work have been explored by sociologists like Diane Vaughan and management historians like James O'Toole.[22] The reasons mainly boil down to the institutional and cultural pressure on companies that keeps them focused on expedience and rapid results. For self-regulation to work, companies would have to modify their senior decision making to weigh all four logics of power simultaneously. This requires concurrent short-term and long-term thinking.

To navigate the boundary between self-regulation and government oversight, AI auditors will likely become more commonplace. As with financial reporting, auditing provides a way to assure all stakeholders of the company's value.

The Four Logics at Play

Corporate logic suggests that businesses should not be accountable to anyone but their owners and shareholders—and that these companies can control themselves. Engineering logic suggests that accountability is a second-order priority, to be delegated to risk and legal specialists. Government logic suggests that there are legal mechanisms for accountability, with the government trusted to oversee control in the form of regulation. Social justice logic suggests that we are all—companies, technologists, and governments alike—accountable to those individuals affected by negative outcomes, especially those who have less control. Decision makers need to think about all four of these logics simultaneously as they set the course for Triple-A systems.

The most obvious starting point for change is within Big Tech. They are at the locus of control, and corporations are often in the habit of avoiding accountability.

> *"We talk about the customer's needs. But there's not much of an organizational conversation around the many ways the technology could be deployed, and I think that's the big missing gap."*
>
> —Casey Cerretani

According to Casey Cerretani, that is precisely where there is a gap in accountability: "We talk about the customer's needs," he says. "But there's not much of an organizational conversation around the many ways the technology could be deployed, and I think that's the big missing gap."

For engineers like Cerretani, this would be as much an ethical conversation as a technological one. Taking facial-recognition software as an example, Cerretani acknowledges that it's needed for many use cases. "By marrying the ethical mindset to that of engineering," he says, "we could add some humanity around the technology."[23] The most critical organizational conversation, he says, doesn't happen—the conversation about how to translate social justice concerns about how the technology will be used and how it might affect people. To operationalize this concern would mean taking cradle-to-grave responsibility for the use of products—not just telling customers what to do with their AI systems, but following through and making sure they do it.

Think of accountability as a constraint and also a form of control—a necessary one to encourage prosocial behavior. If it's a tight, steel grip that punishes those who make mistakes, it will hold back legitimate experimentation, including the kinds of data-based models that helped humanity come to terms with the pandemic. If it's loose and feather-light, it will allow crime to flourish. Imagine instead a system that holds organizations accountable for the technology they create and deploy, rather than simply placing blame on operators—and that prevents criminals and bad actors from misusing Triple-A systems, without constraining their beneficial side.

"Typically, with ethics, everyone is supposed to do good things and avoid bad things, and there's an agreement to sign off on," says Marc Rotenberg. "But in the policy and legal world, we don't think that way. We try to assign rights and responsibilities. Those assignments are typically asymmetric: We place responsibilities purposefully on the organization, companies, and operators that choose to deploy AI systems; we give rights to those individuals who are subjected to the consequences; and we may actually say certain types of systems should be prohibited. Over the last few years, we have seen these types of global frameworks take hold."

Benchmarking Self-Sustainable Regulation

In the research that led up to this book, Juliette developed a framework for evaluating self-regulation in AI. It lays out four factors that together heavily influence affect how a business or government oversees its Triple-A technology (as shown in figure 3).

The Apex Benchmark, as we call it, shows how different parts of an organization influence one another. Suppose that the profit imperative leads the financial side of the company to treat AI responsibility as a cost center. This will weaken the level of oversight and turn well-intended efforts into "ethics-washing." The company may proclaim its caution, but do the minimum needed to comply with state regulations. Other business units will optimize to match this lowest common denominator. They may pretend to be innovative, looking for ways to hold themselves accountable but just ticking the boxes. They may comply with guidelines for acceptable risk but not gather the data needed to actually monitor real risks to people from the technology.

The benchmark also applies to the AI industry as a whole by showing how the lowest common denominator in self-regulation tends to be adopted by all. Typically, if one influential company

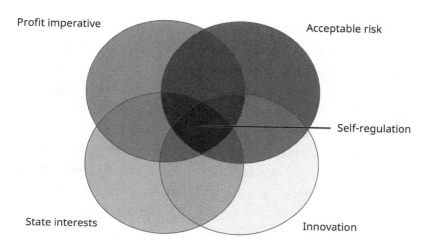

Profit imperative

Acceptable risk

Self-regulation

State interests

Innovation

FIGURE 3 The Apex Benchmark
Source: Juliette Powell, AI self-regulation research, Columbia University, May 13, 2020.

does little to self-regulate, it acts like an apex predator, controlling resource density and restricting smaller predators, who then try and follow suit. The businesses with higher standards look around and see others cutting corners without consequence. They feel foolish for spending extra money and doing the necessary work. If self-regulation is seen to add expense and delay, then the competitor that does the least will win. Standards fall for the entire ecosystem of technology companies.

Companies can also apply this benchmark to develop more effective self-regulation. In practice, this often means reconsidering the pressure to fulfill the profit imperative. That's not easy. Fiduciary responsibility to shareholders is typically mandated by corporate law, except in the very few companies incorporated under "for-benefit" rules. The personal income of the CEO and other top executives depends on rising shareholder value. Even when CEOs propose long-term investment in self-regulation, for the sake of the company's reputation and to reach loftier goals, decision makers throughout the company typically assume that these visionary statements are just rhetoric; it is their job to make the numbers, as it always has been.

To overcome these barriers, the Apex Benchmark tells us to combine the four elements. We foster accountability by making long-term investment a priority for future profits. We establish a shared view of acceptable risk—for the company, its customers, and everyone affected by the products. We sharpen our understanding of state interests and how to further the general welfare. Most of all, we develop research and development teams who follow the engineering logic, but now consider accountability as an integral part of their job.

We do this by using tools and practices that build new collective habits.

Tools for Accountability

How do we keep all stakeholders accountable? The best response we received when asking this question came from Cathy O'Neil: "[A trustworthy system] would treat data science as a science rather than a faith. In practice, that means having evidence, testing hypotheses, making completely clear definitions, understanding the ethical conundrums that a given system has implicitly embedded, considering external as well as internal stakeholders and what their needs and fears are, and monitoring external harms, as well as internal failures."[24]

A more formal approach is through standards. Standards are often seen as mundane and mechanical. They have traditionally been upheld by technological associations like the Institute of Electrical and Electronics Engineers (IEEE). Here, too, the Institute has moved toward issues of responsibility with its IEEE

P7000X and P7003 standards, developed through 13 working groups of diverse people.

Projects that meet this standard affirm that they follow particular practices, among them "evaluating the training/validating data against inherent bias (unjustified skewness), making sure that the decision criteria used by the algorithm are sufficiently understood to be able to justify why certain users might receive different results than others, and clearly documenting scope of use cases for which the algorithm has been validated."[25]

PwC's AI lead, Anand Rao, suggests five other steps that businesses can take to build the capabilities they need:

1. **Education.** Train people in how to test the quality and fairness of data, splitting information into subsets for training the machine learning algorithm, validating the results, and testing the impact.

2. **Data governance.** Consistently articulate the rights that different stakeholders have over the data. Retain visibility into the data's origins, why it was collected, and how it may be safeguarded.

3. **Model governance.** Monitor the other elements involved in an AI system as well. Use metrics to gauge the accuracy, fairness, and explainability of each new effort. For algorithms that are not explained clearly, require more explicit explanations.

4. **Intellectual property (IP) rights.** Demand and guarantee that both (a) creators who share data and (b) collectors of data can each own the rights to their confidential information and can control how it will be disseminated and used. This is particularly important with cloud platforms that store data outside the company.

5. **Open sourcing.** All parties in a project rely on open-source projects, generally with modular components. Don't infringe on confidentiality or competitive dynamics. Cultivate closer relationships with other players in the field.[26]

Ultimately, the liability insurance industry may step in more consistently to hold parties accountable and minimize risk, as Esther Dyson suggests in the foreword to *The AI Dilemma*. There's a precedent in police insurance. Where social justice activists have failed to reign in dangerous and deadly policing practices, insurers have been increasingly successful. That's because many small to medium-sized law enforcement departments in the US have banded together to create insurance risk pools in view of securing lower rates.

> **Ultimately, the liability insurance industry may step in more consistently to hold parties accountable and minimize risk, as Esther Dyson suggests in the foreword.**

Because of the seven-figure jury awards and settlements since the deaths of Breonna Taylor and George Floyd, insurance firms have been paying those costs forward to their clients. Thus, when it comes to police practices like excessive force, insurers have been exerting their power to curb abuse by sharply raising police and city insurance rates. Penalties for the misuse of facial surveillance by law enforcement or cities is a logical next step.[27]

"I've been doing this for 40 years, and this represents a major shift," said John Chino, a broker who secures insurance for cities and counties in six states. "They are asking lots of very detailed questions. 'Do they use chokeholds? What does their de-escalation training look like?'" Police say that implementing these required changes are the only way to get affordable insurance coverage. If they refuse to minimize risk, the pool of members can oust them.

"The members help police themselves," said Alexander T. Brown, a lawyer who specializes in insurance settlements for civil rights plaintiffs. "It's a joint self-insurance program, and they are motivated to keep the pools solvent because it's the members' own money.[28]

Next, in chapter 7, we will look more closely at the nature of organizations and stakeholder ecosystems: the environments in which AI systems are developed. Specifically, we want to know more about what causes them to enable mistakes, accidents, and disasters.

CHAPTER 7

Favor Loosely Coupled Systems

It began at four o'clock in the morning on March 28, 1979, at Three Mile Island, Pennsylvania. The nuclear reactor was operating at nearly full power when the accident in Unit 2 happened. A secondary cooling circuit malfunctioned and affected the temperature of the primary coolant. This sharp rise in temperature made the reactor shut down automatically. In the second it took to deactivate the reactor's system, a relief valve failed to close. The nuclear core suffered severe damage, but operators couldn't diagnose or deal with the unexpected shutdown of the reactor in the heat of the moment. Inadequate control room instrumentation and insufficient emergency response training proved to be root causes of the nuclear plant's meltdown.

In the wake of the Three Mile Island accident, sociologist Charles Perrow did an analysis of why it had happened. He wanted to anticipate other disasters to come. Were all nuclear plants like ticking time bombs? What other technologies might be particularly risky?

After a few years of research, Perrow published his seminal book *Normal Accidents*. His goal, he said, was to "propose a framework for characterizing complex technological systems such as air traffic, marine traffic, chemical plants, dams, and especially nuclear power plants according to their riskiness."

One factor was complexity: the more components and interactions in a system, the more challenging it is when something goes wrong. With scale comes complexity, whether we are thinking of the technology or the organization that supports it. Imagine you run a start-up where everyone sits in the same loft space. From where you sit, you can easily see what they are all doing. In a large organization, that visibility is lost. The moment a leader can't see the inner workings of the system itself—in this case, the staff activities—complexity rises.

Perrow associated this type of complexity with tech failures. Let's return to the example of the Three Mile Island nuclear power plant: Operators couldn't just walk up to its core and measure the temperature manually, or peek inside to discover there was not enough coolant. Similarly, as an executive in a large company, you can't monitor every employee and see what they're doing all the time without incurring resentment. You have to rely on indirect indicators like performance evaluations and sales results. Large companies also rely on complex information technology (IT) and Triple-A systems for their operations, and externally, they rely on complex supply chains.

Tight and Loose Coupling

Another factor, wrote Perrow, was the coupling of a system: the level of interdependence among components. When systems are both complex and tightly coupled, they are more likely to produce negative unexpected consequences and get out of control, as was the case at Three Mile Island.[1]

Tightly coupled systems have architectures—technological and social—that promote interdependence among their components and often isolation from outside connection. This makes them efficient and self-protective but less robust.

Loosely coupled systems, by contrast, have more open and diverse architectures. Changes in one module, section, or component hardly affect the other components. Each operates somewhat independently of the others. A loosely coupled architecture is easy to maintain and scale. It is also robust, in that problems don't propagate easily to other parts of the system.

Executives who run large organizations tend to favor a tightly coupled system. It is what they know. They grew up in their industries seeing a small number of people making decisions that affect millions of people.

A way to control these tightly coupled complex systems is to decouple them. It may seem at first glance like loosely coupled systems are harder to control, but they can actually offer more control, as you'll see in the following example.

Think of a floor covered with dominoes that are lined up. When you tip one over, it will then, in sequence, knock down the entire array of dominoes. This "domino effect" is a simple example of a tightly coupled system. Now try to stop it once the domino effect is in motion. It's much harder than you would think.

A large company is also generally a tightly coupled system, especially compared to small businesses and local mom-and-pop retailers. If you have a complaint about a local grocery store's product, you can take it back and they'll take it in stride, handling it in a different way for each customer. They have control over their actions. If they work in a large company, or as a franchise, they are tightly coupled to the company's branding and scaled-up procedures—and to one another. Those who want to operate differently from the standard procedures must buck the tightly coupled network.

During the pandemic, we realized just how tightly coupled and interconnected our global supply chains are and how one container ship stuck in the Suez Canal can delay global shipments for months. Many organizations have been looking to create more robust redundancies, effectively loosening the coupling in their supply chains by finding alternate vendors and investing in local sources.

A large social media platform is also a complex and tightly coupled system—an intricate web of countless connected people with many different views and motives. It's hard to know how each will react to any particular meme, but the intensity of the reaction is hard to control. Once the genie (or meme) is out of the bottle, you can't put it back in.

The Formula for Disaster

Organizational sociologist Diane Vaughan became an expert on the way systems can repeatedly engender catastrophe when she heard about the *Challenger* disaster:

> On January 28, 1986, I was one of the millions who heard the news and then watched, riveted, as over and over on TV, NASA's space shuttle *Challenger* rose from the launch pad, then turned, and at the words 'Challenger, go at throttle up,' exploded, pieces raining down into the ocean. Lost were seven NASA astronauts, one of them Christa McAuliffe, the teacher in space. The collective shock continued as the presidential commission investigating the accident began its public hearings. They identified the technical cause as a failure of the rubber O-rings to seal the shuttle's solid rocket booster joints. But the NASA organization also failed.[2]

The presidential commission set up to investigate found that NASA had been launching space shuttles with damaged O-rings since 1981. Pressured by the launch schedule, the agency leaders had ignored engineers' warnings right up to the day of the launch. In fact, within the established rules, the agency had labeled the O-ring damage an "acceptable risk."

During the next five years, Vaughan researched and wrote an in-depth book about the organizational problems leading to the technological disaster. Like Perrow, she concluded that this type of organization would repeatedly produce catastrophic mistakes: "[After my book's publication] I heard from engineers and people in many different kinds of organizations who recognized the analogies between what happened at NASA and the situations at their organizations. 'NASA is us,' some wrote."[3]

Another crash, this time of the space shuttle *Columbia*, occurred on February 1, 2003. Another seven astronauts died. A technical review found a piece of foam had broken off and struck a wing. Once again, engineers had warned the agency and the warnings had been ignored. Once again, Vaughan became closely involved in investigating the causes, ultimately joining the government's Columbia Accident Investigation Board (CAIB). She testified to the board that her extensive interviews and other research had found the same organizational causes for both accidents.

In her writing on the disasters, Vaughan cites Perrow in her book, noting that NASA's tightly coupled, complex nature made it systematically prone to occasional major errors. The key decision makers had fallen prey to a "normalization of deviance," in which dangerous complacency gradually became the ordinary way of doing things:

We can never totally resolve the problem of complexity, but we have to be sensitive to our organizations and how they work. While many of us work in complex organizations, we don't realize how much the organizations that we inhabit completely inhabit us. This is as true for those powerful actors at the top of the organization responsible for creating culture as it is for the people in the tiers below them who carry out their directives and do the everyday work.[4]

With the organization like NASA at that time, noted in her testimony, "the technological failure was a result of NASA's organizational failure."[5]

Why AI Is Tightly Coupled

Steve Crandall, a former Bell Labs physicist and founding member of the technology research firm Omenti, shared this observation:

> One feature of our society is an increased [tightening in the] coupling of systems. Social media and other targeted messaging, GPS, the Internet of Things, globalization, just-in-time everything, religion, democracy . . . more systems are being connected, and the amount of communication is increasing at a terrific rate. These couplings are often introduced to decrease cost and the 'friction' [that] parts of the system have with each other. Many [over-coupled] systems are too complex to understand well, but the basic math of over-coupled systems is clear. These systems can be very unstable.[6]

In other words, in Perrow's parlance, negative unintended consequences or "normal accidents" can be expected to increase over time in such systems. This is particularly true for cases where the AI system itself and the organizational ecosystem around it are both complex and tightly coupled.

If you want to make the system safer and less harmful, you have to loosen it up.

Perrow did not include artificial intelligence (AI) or even software among the technologies whose interactions he charted. However, using the criteria that he laid out relative to technological risk, AI systems fit in Perrow's framework next to nuclear power plants, space missions, and DNA sequencing. If something in the Triple-A system isn't working according to plan, there can be unanticipated cascading effects that affect parts of or the entire system in wholly unexpected ways.[7]

Some computer scientists have been exploring the implications of Perrow's theory. Responsible AI software designer Alan Chan, for example, argues that some innate aspects of AI tend to make everything it touches more complex and more tightly coupled.

Even when a project is supposed to be "responsible AI," working with an automated algorithm can override the best intentions of the software engineers. "Although designers may try as much as possible to include all the relevant features, they may only come to know the relevance of some features after an accident informs them to that effect," Chan told us from his home in Canada. "Moreover, while a human observer is limited by the ways in which their senses interact with measurement instruments, an AI subsystem is limited not only by the same conditions as the human observer but also by the fact that human observers select the features for consideration. The measurement instruments may themselves be faulty, which was a crucial factor in the Three Mile Island accident."[8]

These issues do not just affect machine learning (ML) systems. Humans also may not be attentive to all the relevant details and may indeed suffer from information overload. At the same time, the ideal solution is not to trade in human limitations for ML limitations but rather to try to overcome both.

In the tech arena, the process of optimization itself exacerbates tight coupling, says Chan. It creates strong dependencies and, therefore, ripple effects. Imagine an AI system tasked with allocating production resources in a supply chain. The system might have maximizing output as its only goal. This single focus would influence the whole system to couple itself more tightly.

The algorithm would resolve any trade-offs between flexibility and optimization in favor of optimization. For instance, it would not keep reserve stocks because that would drag on inventory. The system is coded to align with the company's strategy in doing this, but in such a tightly coupled way that the system would falter under stress, as many supply chains did at the start of the Covid-19 pandemic. At various times in recent history, this dynamic led to shortages in things like protective equipment, semiconductor chips, diapers, and infant formula.

Another case of a tightly coupled AI system is Zillow's failed use of an automated decision-making algorithm to purchase homes. As an online real estate marketplace, Zillow was originally designed to help sellers and buyers make more informed decisions. In 2018, it opened a new division with a business model based on buying and flipping homes, using a machine learning algorithm called Zillow Offers. As home prices quickly rose during the Covid-19 pandemic, Zillow's iBuying algorithms used data such as the home's age, condition, and zip code to predict which homes would grow in value. However, the system failed to take into account the radical uncertainty caused by the virus and completely underestimated rapid changes in the housing market. Moreover, there was a backlash against Zillow when a real estate agent, Sean Gotcher, created a viral video decrying the company's perceived manipulation of the housing market. By November 2021, the firm sold only 17,000 homes out of the 27,000 it had purchased.

Decoupling Zillow's home-buying business from its online marketplace may have saved the company or at least part of its reputation. Ultimately, Zillow shut down its home-buying division, cut 25 percent of the company's workforce—about 2,000 employees—and wrote off a loss of $304 million in housing inventory.[9]

With AI, Alan Chan argues that the greatest risk lies in AI systems that are both tightly coupled and complex within organizations that are tightly coupled and complex. Big Tech comes to mind. Accidents are especially likely to occur over time when the organizational conditions are right. Since exact conditions cannot be predicted or prevented in detail and the organizational structure prevents them from being resilient, Triple-A systems represent a continual challenge. Even when systems are working well, it is impossible to make them absolutely fail-safe from a "normal accident."

"If I can't look inside the system and see the weights given to different factors, then it is de facto tightly coupled. From a semantic standpoint, I am not given access to the assumptions going in, or how it works. I either have to reject it or use it—those are my only two choices."

—John Sviokla

To John Sviokla, who holds a Harvard doctorate in management information systems, tight coupling is directly related to the opaque nature of algorithmic systems—the closed-box effect we described in chapter 3: "If I can't look inside the system and see the weights given to different factors," he says, "then it is de facto tightly coupled. From a semantic standpoint, I can't communicate with it. I can only manage it by trying to figure out how it works, based on the behaviors it produces. I am not given access to the assumptions going in, or how it works. I either have to reject it or use it—those are my only two choices."[10]

Pixar: A Loosely Coupled Studio

Pixar Animation Studios, the creators of the films *Toy Story* and *Finding Nemo*, has a well-known ritual that takes advantage of the studio's loosely coupled nature. Whenever a film under development hits a rough spot, the director can convene the company's "brain trust" for an in-depth critique. It takes a thick skin to have a work under review, but the result is immense, tangible improvement. Pixar cofounder Ed Catmull explained the process in a *Harvard Business Review* article:

> [The screening] is followed by a lively two-hour give-and-take discussion, which is all about making the movie better. There's no ego. Nobody pulls any punches to be polite. This works because all the participants have come to trust and respect one another. They know it's far better to learn about problems from colleagues when there's still time to fix them than from the audience after it's too late. The problem-solving powers of this group are immense and inspirational to watch.

After the session, says Catmull, the director and his team decide what to do with the advice.

There are no mandatory notes, and the brain trust has no authority. This dynamic is crucial. It liberates the trust members, so they can give their unvarnished expert opinions, and it liberates the director to seek help and fully consider the advice. It took us a while to learn this. When we tried to export the brain trust model to our technical area, we found at first that it didn't work. . . . As soon as we said, 'This is purely peers giving feedback to each other,' the dynamic changed, and the effectiveness of the review sessions dramatically improved [for our technical teams].[11]

Note that the organizational design of the studio is deliberately loose. The brain trust reactions are not treated as demands but as creative opportunities. These opportunities allow for simplicity on the other side of complexity.

Designer Bran Ferren, who has been awarded 500 patents or pending patents, also designed his creative studio Applied Minds to be loosely coupled. This design allows his team to focus on solving complex problems like designing Space Force headquarters.

According to Ferren, "Applied Minds functions more like an atelier or a movie studio model than like a typical requirements-driven engineering or design innovation group within a company. Our project managers are like directors—they're brought in to drive an endeavor from start to finish, recruiting and managing other people to play their parts. It's hard to make that work in large companies that believe in consensus management. Only a few creative companies, like Apple or Disney, work this way. They are led by talented people driving the creative development process and personally deciding what will work. Like Steve Jobs at Apple, this model is very multidisciplinary and talent-driven. You don't set up teams that operate through consensus.

You pick and empower an individual 'talent star,' or they pick themselves and create the company, and you're making the bet on his or her success."[12]

Tools for Simplifying and Loosening Systems

Charles Perrow devoted much of his book *Normal Accidents* to a study of solutions: of those complex sociotechnical operations that had not ended in crisis or catastrophe.

One option is to make decision making simple by focusing on just one or two activities. You centralize decision making around this relatively simple set of goals so that there is clear direction for channeling all the complexities involved.

The second alternative is to loosen the system. Bring decision making to the lowest possible level in the hierarchy, and make sure every part of the organization can operate autonomously. Encourage people to communicate freely, so that no one small group is seen as the single source of knowledge about a key issue.

A third option is to put in place some basic organizational designs. A risk audit and oversight group may seem like yet another boring bureaucratic function, but if it is led by someone who understands loose coupling, then it will be staffed by a diverse group of people who make sense of complex issues together.

If your organization is tightly coupled and you need to make it more loosely coupled, design some inflection points: events where you announce changes in the practices and reporting arrangements. These could be design sessions where you involve everyone in decentralizing their part of the workflow.

"In complex systems," says Steve Crandall, "increasing the coupling produces a change in the systems behavior. In some of the systems we construct, interactions become easier and faster. We see it everywhere, from global shipping systems to GPS tracking on our cell phones.

"Then the system reaches a critical inflection point where everything suddenly changes. It is between difficult and impossible to predict exactly what the new state looks like. That depends on the details of the system and some external elements. For example, when the spread of the Covid-19 virus passed a certain level, we suddenly learned that global shipping and manufacturing systems were brittle."[13]

Move decision making as close as possible to the point of action. Then relentlessly support skill and attitude development that leads to good decisions. Bring people together regularly to learn from each other and avoid competing with other silos. Relentlessly support the kind of leadership development that leads to better decision making, more engaging leadership skills, and attitudes with a broader perspective.

The best tools for organizational change vary depending on the type of organization and the circumstances. To be effective, they all require shifts in attitude among leaders and key people throughout the organization—and among its constituents. That's where creative friction comes in.

CHAPTER 8

Embrace Creative Friction

Imagine that your child comes home from first grade enthralled with a new activity watch that was given out in gym class. Throughout the day, the watch collects data on your child's heart rate, body temperature, sleep patterns, and movement, including the calories expended through exercise. It uses that data to tell wearers of the watch how to manage their weight and grow stronger. It also aggregates that data for analysis by the school administration and the educational research project group (a part of the US Department of Education) that funded the app.[1]

The program is well-intentioned. Its goal is to combat childhood obesity, an increasingly widespread problem. To that end, the whole experience is as seamless and instantaneous as can be. There is no device to buy, no software to install, no contract to sign. Your child says yes simply by accepting it during class. Children don't have to remember to put it on or take it off; the letter to parents from the school's supervisor of health and phys ed says that your little ones should wear it even when sleeping and showering.

However, the experience isn't so seamless if you're a college professor like Brett Frischmann or Evan Selinger, specializing in Internet law, business ethics, and privacy. In their 2018 book *Re-Engineering Humanity*, Frischmann and Selinger tell the story of one real case like this and describe a slippery slope leading to abuse.

Even if the original purpose of the program is defensible, the whole process is targeted to vulnerable populations (in this case, children). Neither the children nor the parents are told exactly what data is being collected, how it is being used, and what protections exist against it being misused. The whole project treats independent evidence gathering, thought, and judgment as mental friction that should be smoothed away. Otherwise, it could keep the project from moving forward.

The child's father, who was one of the authors, ended up "going ballistic." There were so many concerns. Parents were not consulted. There were privacy issues with no way to keep control of children's data. There were no consent forms or ways to opt out, all of which contributed to the opacity of the process. The project was based on complacent acceptance of the surveillance of children throughout their day, including bath and bedtime. Finally, the project cast any parent who objected as a villain to their own child:

> I remembered how my son had come home so excited. The smile on his face and joy in his voice were unforgettable. It was worse than a phishing email scam. They had worked him deeply, getting him hooked. He was so incredibly happy to have been selected, to be part of this new fitness program, to be a leader. How could a parent not be equally excited? Most were, but not me.[2]

The father objected—first to the school administration and Parent-Teacher Association (PTA) and ultimately in a series of meetings with the school's general counsel. The school officials, who had received a $1.5 million PEP grant to beta-test this data-gathering technology, agreed to improve by introducing better disclosure and informed consent forms. According to Frischmann and Selinger, that was the only institutional outcome—an inadequate one.

Imagine if that were your child. Would you have been concerned? If so, would you have thought the issues through and weighed the pros and the cons? Would you have simply ignored it, saying nothing and going with the flow? If you did think it through, would you have consciously acquiesced, not wanting to deprive your child of the program? Would you have taken the extra steps to opt out of the watch program and potentially ostracized your child at school? Or would you have used this dilemma as an opportunity to join others in public dialogue about it? If you took this last option, then you would be introducing creative friction: stepping back to raise collective awareness of the situation and to try to change the way it works.

Friction and the Illusion of Control

Though the school activity watch program was essentially a research program for gathering data about children's health, its consent practices were more like consumer services, where minimal friction is a competitive advantage. In consumer interface design, friction is typically described as "any point in the customer's journey with a company where they hit a snag that slows them down or causes dissatisfaction."[3]

Now that we live in a Triple-A world, we have more options for frictionless experience every day—and the more we get, the more we seem to crave the illusion of control that it gives us.

When that happens, businesses may lose their customers' repeat business—and thus corporate logic focuses on friction-lessness as a path to profitability, closely linked with "customers-for-life" strategies. Consumer-oriented marketers strive to be convenient, to offer choices with focused simplicity, and to make it easier to opt in than opt out. It works, as long as people like the immediate results, and it also reinforces the illusion of being in control. Now that we live in a Triple-A world, we have more options for frictionless experience every day—and the more we get, the more we seem to crave the illusion of control that it gives us.

The idea of creative friction has a long heritage in addressing fears and hopes about technology. Creative friction is deliberate activity designed to break heedless momentum or autopilot. That typically means fostering open, in-depth communication among people with diverse perspectives on a project. When we embrace creative friction, our intent is not to stop progress, but to raise awareness of the negative effects and redirect innovation more thoughtfully, toward more broadly beneficial goals. The eighteenth-century economist Adam Smith, known for the invisible hand of capitalism, proposed a form of creative friction which he called the "impartial spectator." It was the habitual frame of mind of considering every action as if you were seeing someone else do it—what would you think? He described this frame of mind as a way to stop the exploitation which he had seen in early capitalism—for example, the British East India Company's abuses in South Asia.[4]

Philosopher Hannah Arendt, in her 1958 book *The Human Condition*, explicitly referred to a similar form of creative friction in the context of atomic bombs and automation. She wrote that humanity had been saved, in the past, by the constraints of tradition. Most people were limited in what they could do or consider doing. Now, however, there were many more choices. Like choice expert Sheena Iyengar would later point out, Arendt suggested that people, especially those who wield power, are not primed for this much choice.

"Thoughtlessness—the heedless recklessness or hopeless confusion or complacent repetition of 'truths' which have become trivial and empty—seems to me among the outstanding characteristics of our time," she wrote. Her concept of thoughtlessness seems to resemble the frictionlessness that Triple-A systems encourage with the same illusion of control involved. "What I propose, therefore, is very simple," Arendt continued, "it is nothing more than to think what we are doing."[5]

The point of creative friction is not just to consider our actions intellectually, but to be more thoughtful in real time as we act. By embracing creative friction, we avoid doing some things that would harm ourselves or others, or that would create unacceptable risk. We draw people into dialogues about it. We apply discipline to what we say and do, and we accept the annoyances and costs that come with friction. We thus overcome the addictive illusion of control. We make it possible to live with automated technologies in a less risky, more broadly inclusive, more life-affirming way.

Why Frictionlessness Is Addictive

Consider the bargain you make when you click the "Accept Cookies" button to view content online. If you don't click "Accept," you can probably find that information elsewhere, but there is a lot more effort involved in the search. You may even have to do without the content altogether.

Saying no to automated systems generally requires those micro-efforts. If you say no to autofill, you'll have to type your own information all the way through. If you eschew auto-writing assistants, you'll have to compose your own email or reports instead of using AI.

The appeal of frictionlessness is richly documented in business literature—for example, in biographies of Jeff Bezos or books about customer experience.[6] In a 2013 *New Yorker* article on Silicon Valley's culture, journalist George Packer described visiting an entrepreneur who proposed "living in the future" with services like ordering takeout food while riding home in an Uber, timed so that the delivery would arrive just as he did.

Packer could tell that services of this kind would rapidly become commonplace, but the goal of frictionlessness would never be fully reached: "It evokes a fantasy in which all inefficiencies, annoyances, and grievances have been smoothed out of existence. . . . It suddenly occurred to me that the hottest tech start-ups are solving all the problems of being twenty years old, with cash on hand, because that's who thinks them up."[7]

This might seem like a phenomenon limited to wealthy neighborhoods in wealthy countries, but the drive to reduce friction occurs in other places, sometimes to an even greater extent. There are start-ups throughout China and India offering one touch digitally enhanced delivery and travel services: explicitly designed as ways of reducing friction in places where it is not always easy to get around.[8]

The increasingly frictionless nature of digital systems may not be addictive in itself, but it appears to accentuate the craving for feeling in control. There's a reason Steve Krug's popular handbook of web interface design, now in its third edition, is called *Don't Make Me Think*.[9]

Friction and the Logics of Power

The corporate logic associates friction with bureaucracy. Whether friction comes from inside or outside the company, it is seen as an irritation, slowing down innovation and reducing productivity. Ever since Frederick Taylor first codified scientific management in the nineteenth century, the reduction of friction in the factory has been a source of corporate legitimacy.[10] With the introduction of "labor saving" appliances in the twentieth century, reducing friction became a mainstay of consumer marketing. The embrace of AI systems continues this trajectory. They appeal to corporate logic, in part, because they reduce the friction of knowledge work.

The engineering logic often sees friction as a distraction. Many people are eager to delegate questions of AI responsibility to others they see as more qualified. Governments understand friction—they have a lot of experience with it—but as we saw in chapter 6 with the Netherlands story, there is always a temptation to take shortcuts and override resistance. Triple-A systems give governments far more power to do so.

Even social justice activists may shrink back at times from the friction of genuine dialogue with people who hold other perspectives. We see this at times online and when students protest speeches they don't agree with.

Dialogue among all these groups is essential, and dialogue involves friction. Brett Frischmann and Harvard-based free speech advocate Susan Benesch call this type of dialogue "friction-in-design," and suggest it as a component of government regulation.[11] It requires people to come to a frame of mind where they genuinely pay attention to what other people think and why they think what they do. One reason for creative friction now, for bringing diverse thinkers together to address the complexities of

AI, is because we need the practice. We haven't all worked together enough, and we don't yet have the trust or empathy that we will need. Creative friction is a tool to use rather than something to avoid.

Tools for Creative Friction

Cultivating creative friction within your organization means adding broader, more diverse perspectives, deeper judgments, time for thoughtful evaluation, and ongoing review—all embedded within the development and deployment of Triple-A systems and integral to all of it. For many people, this will seem like extra work or an impossible task. It does not feel good at first to add friction if you are used to frictionlessness. Nonetheless, to achieve results in which AI systems benefit far more groups of people, some form of creative friction is ongoing and necessary during the conception, development, and deployment of the technologies.

In the rest of this chapter we will look at people and organizations that have deliberately introduced creative friction to accomplish real-world tasks—including impossible tasks.

For example, Astro Teller is the cofounder and Captain of Moonshots at X, also known as the Moonshot Factory. X is a creative laboratory for groundbreaking ideas and "moonshot" innovations—efforts to address fundamental problems facing humanity with solutions that must also be commercially viable. Since the lab was launched by Google in 2010, X has created projects and companies such as Waymo (autonomous vehicles), Chorus (digital transformation of supply chains), Malta (energy storage), and Tapestry (dynamic models of the electric power grid). One deep learning research project, Google Brain, has powered Google Translate, YouTube's video recommendations, and more.

To explain how he creates an environment in which creative friction flourishes, Teller has said, "Innovators and dreamers often can't thrive in typical organizations. Their constant 'what ifs' and 'why does it have to be this way' can be irritating for organizations trying to lock in an execution plan and meet quarterly targets. . . . Don't get me wrong—execution matters, especially when you're operating at scale. But radical innovation needs a different cultural environment than product delivery does."[12]

Indeed, by many accounts, X does have a different cultural environment than most innovation labs, even in Silicon Valley. X is different from its corporate parent Google. It reminds some observers of places like the original Bell Labs and Xerox Palo Alto Research Center (PARC). Organizations like X produce constantly, but always with an interest in making sense of what they're doing and why they are choosing particular projects to work on. Teams invite one another to collaborate, especially if they come from different research backgrounds, and they ask tough questions that require well-considered answers.

David Stark found a similar approach to creative friction in his studies of entrepreneurial companies and Wall Street teams. According to Stark,

> Success requires attention to . . . a collective sense of rhythm and timing—of when to make temporary settlements to get the job done, with the knowledge that this is not a once-and-for-all resolution of the disagreements. . . . [This way of settling decisions] is neither harmony nor cacophony but an organized dissonance. . . . In highly uncertain and rapidly changing environments the key challenge is . . . how to develop practices so that you will not take your knowledge for granted.[13]

There is a common thread to the various practices that businesses—from startups to large companies—use to develop creative friction. They generally require changes in the way people think and interact. "Our breakthrough idea [at X] isn't a technology," explains Teller in all earnestness, "it's our people. It's about engineering a culture and designing an organization that can overcome the powerful forces that cause humans to retreat to the comfortable and conventional."[14]

Practice Collaborative Conflict

Firms that cultivate creative friction routinely hire people who can confront one another's ideas. They bring in outside experts to challenge internal teams as a form of collaborative conflict. Harvard Business School professor Dorothy Leonard refers to constructive argument as creative abrasion.

> If you want an innovative organization, you need to hire, work with, and promote people who make you uncomfortable.... The biggest barrier to recognizing the contributions of people who are unlike you is your own ego. Suppose you are stuck on a difficult problem. To whom do you go for help? Usually to someone who is on the same wavelength or to someone whose opinion you respect. These people may give you soothing strokes, but they are unlikely to help spark a new idea.
>
> Suppose you were to take the problem instead to someone with whom you often find yourself at odds, someone who rarely validates your ideas or perspectives. It may take courage and tact to get constructive feedback, and the process may not be exactly pleasant. But that feedback will likely improve the quality of your solution. And when your adversarial colleague recovers

from their amazement at your request, they may even get along with you better because the disagreement was clearly intellectual, not personal.[15]

The Studio X innovation studio, an incubator launched by Shell Oil in 2014, explicitly frames creative abrasion as a team practice needed for conflict-averse cultures, especially in start-ups. There are ground rules for teams, like requiring people to actively listen. Participants challenge each other, rather than just stating their own ideas.[16]

From 2002 through 2014, Juliette worked with Cirque du Soleil as an outside consultant on special projects, working with then-creative director Jean-Francois Bouchard. "La Création" is the term generally used to describe their process of creating new shows, events, and derivative products. In Cirque parlance, "La Création" means creative friction. Guy LaLiberté, the founder and visionary behind Cirque, would typically define the theme of each new show. Sometimes two words like "Michael Jackson" would open the door to the creative process. Then Cirque's culture of innovation and creativity would kick in, encouraging exploration, honesty, and good judgment. Passionate, provocative, and at times chaotic creative disagreements led to more innovative ideas and technologies. Instead of consensus, we were seeking multidisciplinary collaboration and breakthroughs.

David Stark found that organizations that followed this type of friction were less efficient in the short run but ultimately benefited from taking the time to question and challenge each other. In entrepreneurial business cultures, friction among teammates is up close and personal. People with opposite points of view directly interact and insist on working together, project after project.

"People argued," wrote Stark. "They gave reasons and provided justifications as they attempted to persuade others about the things they valued.... True, they needed to settle their differences to meet their project deadlines. But...these settlements were provisional, beneath which were profound disagreements and misunderstandings that would come to the fore once again."[17]

Use Diversity of Thinking as a Catalyst

Diverse and multidisciplinary teams generate creative friction. Diversity here means diversity of thought, culture, gender, and ability; it also means socioeconomic diversity, diversity in education, and neurodiversity. As entrepreneur and parallel computing pioneer Danny Hillis puts it, creative friction that leads to innovation requires diversity in all of its forms.

> When I went to Disney, I got to see the way that Hollywood does innovation—the studio system. When you see a Disney film, it's not made mostly by people who are employees of Disney. Disney just acts as the catalyst. They put together the project with lots of outside talent, which means they get much more diversity of people working on a project, and that keeps them from making the same movie over and over and over again.

Hillis has founded or cofounded a number of renowned tech-related organizations. In many of them, he deliberately recreates the friction-generating structure—diverse people coming together for projects—that he had enjoyed at Disney.

> I wanted to have a group that worked on interdisciplinary innovation, in a studio setting. Today, we have a core of a few hundred project managers who cut across technical areas. So, there

might be somebody who's done both electrical engineering and mechanical engineering or has done both chemistry and biology and who also has the ability to make something from scratch. And then we have a big network of people who are specialists that have deep knowledge.[18]

In assembling your own diverse group, include diverse stakeholders who will be affected by the technology. Before you build anything, they can help you think it through. Make sure you incorporate the thinking of social scientists, community leaders, academics, and scientists, as well as technologists.

Remember that not everybody is comfortable saying something out loud. They may participate in a chat window instead. Collaborative technology can help enable a broader representation of viewpoints.

The virtuous feedback loop of incorporating community response into your project is not just a one-time thing. Ongoing feedback allows minimum viable products to improve over time. Ask for feedback and incorporate it at every stage of development and after deployment. This ensures that your team has on-the-ground knowledge of the impact and that possibilities for improvement are not left on the table. Moreover, it creates a space for evaluating any potential harms of the technology on people well before they escalate into a crisis.

David Stark studied trading teams on Wall Street and in Japan. In both places, he found that teams with people with diverse backgrounds and viewpoints performed better than their less diverse counterparts. The teams asked many more questions when they had a diverse group than when they had a homogeneous group. Decisions took longer to make, but in the medium and the long run the teams ended up making far more money.

The key element in diversity, Stark found, was "competing orders of worth": different perspectives on what is valuable.[19] The four stakeholder logics in this book, for instance, represent four different ideas about what matters. Business leaders value ownership, markets, and growth; engineers value efficiency and technological capabilities; social justice advocates value fairness and equity, especially for the vulnerable; and governments value service, protection, and control. All organizations have their own internal conflicts based on their own competing orders of worth.

Cirque du Soleil explicitly orients itself around diverse teams. Cirque founder Guy LaLiberté was a fire-breather when he started out; along with his busker friends in Baie-Saint-Paul, Quebec, he consciously chose to foster a culture that welcomes and encourages artistic tension and disruption through diversity. For as long as Juliette worked with them, creating special projects and events, she was always amazed by the variety of people working there. Officially, Cirque employs performers from over 50 countries in its Montreal headquarters. Juliette was one of the lucky ones who, in addition to finding solutions to creative and business problems for Cirque, also helped them adopt even more technology into their shows. The first time Juliette ever experienced an AI-driven drone swarm was in the context of a Cirque du Soleil show. Cirque is always on the lookout to recruit new artists, technologists, and creators. This diversity of people, thinking, vision, culture, and technologies is core to the creative friction and cross-disciplinarian tension that feeds world-class ideas and cutting-edge innovation. As a result, Cirque has collaborated with a far-ranging group of partners, working to co-create everything from opening ceremonies for the Olympic Games to Madonna World Tours to Broadway shows, in addition to their permanent and touring

Cirque du Soleil branded shows. Moreover, "to keep its creative brand fresh, Cirque works closely with engineering and art departments in 17 universities and actively seeks ideas from students, many of which eventually make it into the shows."[20]

Create Scenarios of Alternative Futures

When it comes to new technology, it is especially important to ask teams to create scenarios of what the future with this tech might look like for the people it is aimed at. Think of several alternative futures that would change the way your Triple-A system could be used. Then ask the communities that will be affected what they think. Incorporate their various perspectives into your scenarios to better understand what the trade-offs are. Under each of those scenarios, how might it benefit people? In what ways could it cause unforeseen harm in the short, medium, and long term? What approaches could you take now that would make the system more beneficial to more people, no matter which scenario unfolds?

Ask these different groups to come together and weigh in on a risk–benefit analysis before new technologies or new use cases are deployed and, ideally, before systems are designed. This process will help generate the kind of risk thinking that Ron Dembo proposes (see chapter 2) when we write about hedging against radical uncertainty.

The story of the child who received a smartwatch suggests another way to develop scenarios: focusing on the future we would want to create. Authors Frischmann and Selinger proposed an alternative future of participative learning about the watch's provenance and implications. "Fitness and privacy might be joined as students learn about the technology and their relationships to it and to others (the school, the Department of Education, device manufacturers, various third parties including aggregators and advertisers)."[21] Students might even discover the value of real control over their devices, health, and personal data.

Fail Fast, Fail Forward

X, Pixar, Disney, and Cirque du Soleil regularly conduct premortems and post-mortems. Take X's "bad idea brainstorm," in which an innovation session starts by asking people to share the worst ideas they can think of. The purpose is to celebrate having ideas at all, even if they're bad. They are not afraid to kill projects. Indeed, all of these companies use creativity, new technology, and diversity to both create and to kill projects.

"Failing fast and failing forward" happens when you fail quickly in testing out a hypothesis; if you have learned from the experience, you have still failed, but you have failed forward. Or as X's Astro Teller puts it,

> Our main cultural battle is against fear and the strong gravitational pull toward conventional ways of thinking and behaving. All of us have been conditioned for years not to fail, not to be vulnerable, and to minimize risk. So my number one job is helping Xers reset and free themselves from these invisible but pernicious constraints so they can free up their potential.[22]

At X, many rituals involve celebrations of failure. One project involved converting seawater into fuel. When the team decided it wasn't commercially viable and shut down the project, teammates were all given a bonus. The company then held an all-hands meeting to thank them for "speeding up innovation"—by which they really meant drawing back so they could focus on more viable projects.

Create a Safer Environment for Creative Friction

Creative friction requires open discussion, where people feel secure to raise questions and offer different perspectives. Amy Edmondson's work on psychological safety demonstrates how leaders can set a context for people to talk openly and freely without reprisal.[23]

Astro Teller has created an atmosphere of psychological safety at X: "We work hard to create an environment where everyone feels comfortable sharing their views and loves running toward really hard problems precisely because they're difficult."[24]

When you are surrounded by like-minded individuals who have "been there" in terms of repeated failure, you'll feel more understood, heard, and inspired to keep building on what you've learned.

There are other ways to create a supportive learning environment, in part by giving people control over their time. At the X Lab, employees are encouraged to take periods of discovery—shifting temporarily to a different project or just taking time to daydream so that they gain a fresh perspective. They are also trusted to work on projects where they don't have preestablished expertise.

In academia, the rapid introduction of ChatGPT and similar products is bringing creative friction into the classroom. Professors are reworking essay assignments to ask students less about information available on the web, and more about students' personal experience and thoughts.[25]

Be a Model of Creative Friction Yourself

Senior leaders and team members can use their own behavior to show what creative friction looks like. In fact, this practice appears to make people more effective as leaders. One explanation comes from neuroscience research. The brain's center of executive function, which processes impulse control, cognitive complexity, and multiple perspectives, is strengthened when people consider complex issues together in contentious but constructive ways—in other words, through creative friction.[26]

This is particularly relevant for strategic leadership: the ability to lead an organization toward long-term plans and goals. When leaders practice creative friction regularly, in their own behavior or in teams, it reinforces this strategic focus. Conceivably, the use of AI for decision making—especially if people get in the habit of relying on automated systems—might cause our strategic leadership capabilities to atrophy.

Adam Galinsky, a social psychologist at Columbia University, has documented the tendency of leaders in positions of authority to lose perspective. They are more prone than others to take careless risks (for example, divulging sensitive facts in negotiations). As leaders move up the chain of command, they are less likely to consider multiple perspectives or what others are thinking. Another researcher, University of Washington professor Leigh Plunkett Tost, found that the feeling of having power leads people to discount advice from others.[27]

Many times, modeling creative friction takes the form of small behavioral changes. Sociologists Paul DiMaggio and Walter W. Powell refer to these old habits as "taken-for-granted scripts, rules, and classifications—the stuff of which institutions are made."[28] David Andre, the chief science officer at X, disclosed openly to friends and colleagues in 2004 that he had begun to replace the word "but" in his speech pattern with the word "and." He had been practicing this bit of self-regulation over time and noticed how it began to rewire his brain to be more collaborative with his teammates and in his personal life as well.

Lead with Data and Curiosity

Janet Thompson, executive vice president at the data-driven creative agency Performance Art, provides an example of leading with curiosity. Janet attends New York's General Assembly Institution in her spare time, to learn the art of data science by cultivating new skills, like learning to code in Python and query data herself.[29] Entrepreneur David Bankston (chapter 3) also went back to school, to get a bachelor's degree in computer science at Purdue University during the 2020 pandemic.

The key to leading with data and curiosity is the belief that you can figure it out. Often in technology, when you are doing something new, it feels uncomfortable. You feel less confident than you did in your previous job or project. If you believe you can figure it out, you can do it.

Collaboration with the right people is the key. Ask for help. Where you have a knowledge gap, find people to fill that gap. Most important is building a truly excellent diverse team of people who can be candid together. Functional humility emerges when you surround yourself with experts who know things you don't know. You don't have to be the smartest person in the room. It's better to be the person who brought smart people together to collaborate—and who fostered an environment where they feel comfortable talking openly. Then, you strategically become the person at the center of all the action.

Discuss Your Triple-A Systems' Broader Impact

Schedule regular discussions, with the four logics represented, of the outcomes your Triple-A systems will produce. One good discussion template is the "threats and mitigations" framework published in early 2023 by researchers at the Stanford University Internet Observatory, part of its cyber policy center. They worked in partnership with another research group at Georgetown University, along with some people from OpenAI. To develop this framework, they practiced a form of creative friction themselves, bringing together machine learning experts and researchers in online disinformation.

Any team producing an AI system, they say, should consider three factors, especially in developing or using systems that generate text, images, or other content. The goal here is to keep from disseminating false or manipulative information:

1. **Actors:** The people who might use the systems to deliberately mislead others. Their number is expanding rapidly as sophisticated AI systems become available for free or at low cost.
2. **Behavior:** The way these operators could act. For example, operators could scale up and manipulate others with personalized chatbots.
3. **Content:** The new types of propaganda and misleading influence that might proliferate.

Discussions could also cover new capabilities that the AI systems enable, the speed at which they become available, and the pressure that the company could put on users to foster more beneficial "norms." The authors propose discussions at four key moments during the R&D process: When the model is being constructed; when people are given access to it; when content is disseminated; and in a fourth stage called "belief formation," when end users recognize the impact their digital tools are having on their beliefs and behaviors. This last stage is in the realm of digital literacy in the face of consumer-focused AI tools like ChatGPT.[30]

Think through Implications, Not Just Applications

"We decided to tackle the longer, harder path of creating fully self-driving cars instead of launching a partially autonomous 'freeway assistant' feature, because we wanted to help people who couldn't drive at all and make roads as safe as possible."

—Astro Teller

X explicitly gave itself a strategic goal to address some of the world's hardest problems. In communicating this goal, Teller emphasizes that while solutions have to be financially viable, they also have to seek positive outcomes for people in general. "Taking the long view enables us to think through the implications [and] not just the applications of what we're building and ensure we're taking into account the needs of many different people affected by any new technology. For example, [with Waymo], we decided to tackle the longer, harder path of creating fully self-driving cars instead of launching a partially autonomous 'freeway assistant' feature, because we wanted to help people who couldn't drive at all and make roads as safe as possible."[31]

Teams can also explicitly use the unacceptable-risk concept, as described in chapter 1. MIT research scientist Renée Richardson Gosline proposed this concept in a *Harvard Business Review* article: "Perhaps the first and most critical inconvenient act is for your team to take a beat and ask, 'Should AI be doing this? And can it do what is being promised?' Question whether it is appropriate to use AI at all in the context of your use case. For example, it cannot predict criminal behavior and should not be used for 'predictive policing' to arrest citizens before the commission of crimes."

To understand the implications of use cases, Gosline also suggests to "deliberately place kinks in the processes . . . and incorporate 'good friction' touchpoints that surface the limitations, assumptions, and error rates for algorithms. . . . Consider [involving] external AI audit partners that may be less embedded in organizational routines."[32]

Ask yourself and your mix of stakeholders: Are we doing this AI project for the right reason? Is the work really about advancing the mission? Does this project have a healthy relationship with risk?

Be reflective and intentional. History has proved how many great innovations and forward progress has happened when teams continuously remember why they started their projects in the first place.

Conclusion

In the introduction to *The AI Dilemma*, we acknowledged that the technology in the wrong hands is dangerous but in the right hands is beneficial to all. Furthermore, trying to change its trajectory is more difficult than it might seem. As we saw with the Moral Machine experiment, what people want self-driving cars to do is not universal. It changes depending on context, geography, culture, and global zeitgeist—just to name a few factors.

Therefore, what responsible technology means to us right now may not hold over time.

We also cannot control Triple-A systems by figuring out how they work or reverse-engineering their intentions. They are machines. Machines don't have intentions. However, as researcher Iyad Rahwan says, "we can judge them by their behavior."

Rahwan, as you may recall, is the computer scientist at MIT's Media Lab who worked with Edmond Awad on the Moral Machine experiment. In 2018, he coauthored an article with another Media Lab faculty member, Manuel Cebrian, proposing that machine behavior should be an academic discipline. Rahwan drew a cartoon (see figure 4) driving home the point.

Rahwan's cartoon says it all: We can't know if a Triple-A system is responsible or if it perpetuates social inequality by opening the closed box and looking at its source code, any more

FIGURE 4 Opacity of Regulated Machines Is Not New
Source: Iyad Rahwan and Manuel Cebrian, "Machine Behavior Needs to Be an Academic Discipline," *Nautilus*, March 29, 2018. Reprinted with permission from the artist.

than we can be sure that someone is a good person by looking at their clothing or their brain MRI. Despite the name of the MIT experiment, machines are not moral, but they do exhibit behaviors.

Rahwan and Cebrian provide some examples of judging a machine by its behavior. "[When] computer scientists create their agents to solve particular tasks—no small feat—they most often focus on ensuring that their agents fulfill their intended function. For this, they use a variety of benchmark data sets and tasks that make it possible to compare different algorithms objectively and consistently." For example, in the case of email classification programs, the MIT researchers have found that such programs "should meet a benchmark of accuracy in classifying email to spam or non-spam using some 'ground truth' that is labeled by humans." In the case of computer vision algorithms, "they must correctly detect objects in human-annotated image data sets like ImageNet." For autonomous cars, Rahwan and Cebrian would have them "navigate successfully from A to B in a variety of weather conditions." For game-playing agents like AlphaGo, "they must defeat other state-of-the-art algorithms, or humans who won a particular honor—such as being the world champion in chess, Go, or poker."[1]

This doesn't mean Triple-A systems—algorithmic, autonomous, and automated systems—pass the Turing test, at least not today. It means they are complex sociotechnical systems; people and systems are interrelated or tightly coupled—and should be understood as such.

"Machines do not understand—yet," says Columbia professor Marka Szabolcs, the same physicist who is concerned about Triple-A systems managing nuclear weapons. But he also regards them as he would regard a child: "When a child learns, the brain dreams, abstracts, and understands, so it needs fewer examples to get more of the world. Understanding is key to future AI, and we need to understand 'understanding' to get there."[2]

7 Principles for the New Wave of AI Systems

The creative and conversational tools released in late 2022—and later known generically as generative AI—are finding huge audiences. OpenAI launched an AMT called ChatGPT in November 2022, and within three months it had scaled to 100 million users. Google expects an initial user base of about 1 billion for its experimental chatbot, known as Bard. Bard, which is powered by LaMDA, Google's Language Model for Dialogue Applications, will be integrated with Google search, just as Microsoft is integrating OpenAI tools with its search engine Bing. Those who use generative AI say things like, "It's an entirely new way of interacting with information on the internet."[3] These bots and conversational tools apparently fill a deeply-felt need people didn't know they had: a need to gain more control, whether illusory or real, over their ability to find and send information.

It's all happening so quickly that by the time this book is published in summer 2023, we may need to write a sequel. For now, let's think about the ways in which these rapidly expanding AI systems (including their sociotechnical context) could behave in light of the seven principles for responsible technology:

Be Intentional about Risk to Humans: Unlike Meta and Open AI, Google decided not to release its entire advanced language model, LaMDA, to be first to market. Instead, through an app called the AI Test Kitchen, it released carefully curated experiences with little or no risk of disinformation, hate speech, or other harmful effects. Google's LaMDA was trained on open-ended conversations and dialogues.[4]

There was reason to be this intentional. In August 2022, Meta released a chatbot called BlenderBot and over the course of just one weekend, it became nasty. By the third day, it was spewing disinformation. Meta now requires visitors to the BlenderBot demonstration sites to click a box saying: "I understand this bot is for research and entertainment only, and that it is likely to make untrue or offensive statements. If this happens, I pledge to report these issues to help improve future research. Furthermore, I agree not to intentionally trigger the bot to make offensive statements." OpenAI CEO Sam Altman similarly said that users should actively "thumbs down" negative responses and postings from chatbots (including their own ChatGPT), to train them to make better associations over time.[5]

"What's required is a serious look at the architecture, training data and goals. That requires a company to prioritize these kinds of ethical issues a lot more than just asking for a thumbs down."

—Steven T. Piantadosi

These measures place the burden of intentionality on users. That is, at best, a short-lived solution. Already, conversational AI tools appear to be competing, in part, on their ability to avoid producing false and harmful outcomes. If that continues, it will influence Triple-A system design—and if it doesn't continue, it may spark a backlash. "What's required is a serious look at the architecture, training data and goals," says Steven T. Piantadosi, head of the computation and language lab at the University of California, Berkeley. "That requires a company to prioritize these kinds of ethical issues a lot more than just asking for a thumbs down."[6]

Open the Closed Box: It will continue to be difficult to look "under the hood" of machine learning systems like the new conversational AI tools. Explainability will rely on the ability to track information and outcomes. We're starting to see several methods emerge. Google's Responsible AI team maintains a severity analysis of the responsibility risks, including a dollar value calculation of the potential harm to humans. We can imagine auditors, insurers, or regulators creating a liability index, perhaps maintained by AI systems, that updates the risk costs on an ever-changing dashboard—with

Tech companies and users penalized if they don't provide accurate input.

Reclaim Data Rights for People: As we suggested in chapter 4, the idea of managing data rights has been percolating for some time. With generative AI, the possibility of personal AI emerges. What if you had an AI bot of your own that held your information sacrosanct in your own private cloud and negotiated on your behalf with all the other bots? You could see its own guidelines and ask it for clearer explanations when needed. You could say, "I don't want to provide information to this site, but I'd like to access some of its information," and your bot would navigate the necessary access and permissions without carelessly breaching any of your boundaries. If it included a way to monetize access to your data, it might cover the costs of its own use.

Confront and Question Bias: Like previous generations of chatbots, generative AI systems tend to project negative bias—misogyny, discrimination, and offensive content—because they find it in online postings. Textio CEO Kieran Snyder, whose firm consults on inclusive language for workplace communications, tested ChatGPT's tendencies to write racist or sexist performance reviews. A "bubbly receptionist is presumed to be a woman," she noted, "while the unusually strong construction worker is presumed to be a man." OpenAI's ChatGPT had the same tendency and was explicitly trained to correct it. Thus, when people ask for essays on why only white or Asian men would make good scientists, the bot catches it and responds, "It is not appropriate to use a person's race or gender that way."[7]

Hold Stakeholders Accountable: Several companies have developed image generation models like DALL-E and chosen to take their time to release them because of the risk. Their own internal responsibility reviews suggested these programs could be misused to produce deepfakes en masse—generating false and misleading images for political purposes or to abuse someone. For many AI system creators and users, the temptation will be great to delegate this burden to sophisticated conversational AI tools and chatbots. In chapter 6, in the section Just Because Government Can, Doesn't Mean It Should, we asked: "Who watches the watchrobots?" If there are no established overarching gatekeepers, the watchrobots may end up watching one another.

Favor Loosely Coupled Systems: Chatbots may tighten couplings in complex systems, intensifying the communications between them. What happens when Google chatbots encounter Microsoft chatbots—or when ChatGPT has a conversation with Bard? Because of the closed box, we don't know how either one gets their answers. What happens when they start communicating with one another?

Embrace Creative Friction: Companies and governments need a framework for thinking deeply about impact: a calculus of intentional risk. As you develop a new generative AI system, you estimate damages and benefits. What harm can it do? What good can it do for others? What if you break a law? The EU AIA may fine companies up to 6 percent of their total worldwide annual revenues for unacceptable risks. Add reputation loss, then factor in the costs of not releasing it—including the opportunity cost of all that lost business. At the end, we want to be able to look at ourselves in the mirror. We are all wielding immense power, and we need a calculus to keep us from harming ourselves, others, and the bottom line.

Arms Race or Human Race?

The core of the AI dilemma is not the ability of machines to learn. It is the ability of humans to learn to manage the growing abilities of these new systems. To gain real control, instead of illusory control, we need to raise our own awareness and ability first. Like first-time parents discovering the challenges that come with parenthood, we are now discovering that the emergence of AI is a forcing function. It is forcing us, those who operate in any or all of the four logics, to grow up—at least enough to take seriously the responsibility that we have created for ourselves.

Peter Sloly, the former chief of police of the Ottawa police service, phrases the core question this way:

"We especially need to understand what we, as the community of human beings, want to prioritize with AI. Is it for the arms race or for the human race?"

—Peter Sloly

"We especially need to understand what we, as the community of human beings, want to prioritize with AI. Is it for the arms race or for the human race?"

Will our Triple-A systems continue to treat people differently, hurting some people more than others, in different cases and contexts? Will they be held to a benchmark—a standard of responsibility? Who will set that standard, and who will control the outcome?

An academic field of machine behavior is emerging, focused on questions like these.[8] Iyad Rahman is now director of the Center for Humans and Machines at the Max Planck Institute in Berlin, explicitly designed to further this field. There is much to learn about the interrelationship between machine behavior, human behavior, and the behavior of larger sociotechnical systems like corporations and governments.

In the end, it doesn't matter whether we think our AI systems are intelligent or not. What matters most is what they do and how they grow, and how we grow along with them. Like loving parents, we need to keep watch over the systems we are raising. We need to guide them as we would a child toward full adulthood. We need to instill respect for our shared benefit and interdependence. Then, when we let them go, it won't be into a separate, isolated world with them or us in control. It will be into a world where we are all working together to create greater real control for all of us.

Notes

Introduction

1. The Moral Machine website, MIT Media Lab, https://www.moralmachine.net/results/-834773863.

2. Philippa Foot, "The Problem of Abortion and the Doctrine of the Double Effect," *Oxford Review*, no. 5 (1967), https://philpapers.org/archive/FOOTPO-2.pdf; Sara Bizarro, "The Trolley Problem—Origins," *Medium*, (March 16, 2020), https://sarabizarro.medium.com/the-trolley-problem-73e22048d88e.

3. J.-F. Bonnefon, A. Shariff, and I. Rahwan, "The Social Dilemma of Autonomous Vehicles," *Science* 352, no. 6293 (June 24, 2016): 1573–1576, https://www.science.org/doi/abs/10.1126/science.aaf2654; Azim Shariff, Iyad Rahwan, and Jean-François Bonnefon, "Whose Life Should Your Car Save?" *New York Times*, November 3, 2016, https://www.nytimes.com/2016/11/06/opinion/sunday/whose-life-should-your-car-save.html.

4. Edmond Awad and Sohan Dsouza, "Inside the Moral Machine: When Your Experiment Survey Becomes Reaction Video Material," *NaturePortfolio: Behavioural and Social Sciences Community*, October 24, 2018, https://socialsciences.nature.com/posts/40067-inside-the-moral-machine.

5. PewDiePie, "Am I a Good Person?" *YouTube*, video, 10:25, June 14, 2017, https://youtu.be/BGi17Tw_zYQ; jacksepticeye, "Right or Wrong? | Moral Machine," *YouTube*, video, 21:25, January 3, 2017, https://youtu.be/xCeOpOkiS-4; Zombi_Sagan, "Decide Who Lives and Who Dies. The Moral Machine," *Reddit*, October 3, 2016, https://www.reddit.com/r/Futurology /comments/55oagt/decide_who_lives_and_who_dies_the _moral_machine/.

6. Tom Krisher, "11 More Crash Deaths Are Linked to Automated-Tech Vehicles," *Los Angeles Times*, October 18, 2022, https://www.latimes.com/business/story/2022-10-18/11 -more-crash-deaths-are-linked-to-automated-tech-vehicles.

7. E. Awad, S. Dsouza, R. Kim, J. Schulz, J. Henrich, A. Shariff, J.-F. Bonnefon, and I. Rahwan, "The Moral Machine Experiment," *Nature* 563, no. 7729 (2018): 59–64, https://doi.org/10 .1038/s41586-018-0637-6.

8. Tech Desk, "OpenAI's ChatGPT Chatbot Crosses One Million Users in Less than a Week," *Indian Express*, December 10, 2022, https://indianexpress.com/article/technology/tech-news -technology/openai-chatgpt-crosses-1-million-users-ceo-says -they-might-have-to-monetise-this-8306997/.

9. La'Kay Hodge, *Response to the AI Dilemma,* correspondence with the authors, February 3, 2023.

10. Cade Metz, "The New Chatbots Could Change the World. Can You Trust Them?," *New York Times,* December 10, 2022, https://www.nytimes.com/2022/12/10/technology/ai-chat -bot-chatgpt.html.

11. Email correspondence with 3ric Johanson, January–February 2023.

12. Email correspondence with Kevin Kelly, June 2022.

13. Ryan Carrier, executive director of the audit and advocacy group ForHumanity, used the term "Triple-A systems" in an

interview. In ForHumanity's risk management framework, the three "As" are artificial intelligence, algorithmic, and autonomous systems. See "Risk Management," ForHumanity, 2022, https://forhumanity.center/bok/risk-management/.

14. Art Kleiner, "Ellen Langer on the Value of Mindfulness in Business," *Strategy+Business,* February 9, 2015, https://www.strategy-business.com/article/00310.

15. E. J. Langer, "The Illusion of Control," *Journal of Personality and Social Psychology* 32, no. 2, (1975): 311–328, https://doi.org/10.1037/0022-3514.32.2.311.

16. S. C. Thompson, W. Armstrong, and C. Thomas, "Illusions of Control, Underestimations, and Accuracy: A Control Heuristic Explanation, *Psychological Bulletin* 123, no. 2 (1998): 143–161, https://doi.org/10.1037/0033-2909.123.2.143.

17. Olivia Solon, "Ex-Facebook President Sean Parker: Site Made to Exploit Human 'Vulnerability,'" *The Guardian,* November 9, 2017, https://www.theguardian.com/technology/2017/nov/09/facebook-sean-parker-vulnerability-brain-psychology; personal conversation with Sean Parker, John Perry Barlow, and Juliette Powell while attending the E-G8 Summit, a meeting of government and business leaders focused on the internet and global public policy, Deauville, France, May 2011.

18. Lauren A. Leotti, Sheena S. Iyengar, and Kevin N. Ochsner, "Born to Choose: The Origins and Value of the Need for Control," *Trends in Cognitive Sciences* 14, no. 10 (2010): 457–463, https://doi.org/10.1016/j.tics.2010.08.001.

19. The first quote is from our personal interview with Sheena Iyengar, November 2022. The second quote is from Leotti, Iyengar, and Ochsner, "Born to Choose."

20. B. Ricker, N. Schuurman, and F. Kessler, "Implications of Smartphone Usage on Privacy and Spatial Cognition: Academic

Literature and Public Perceptions," *GeoJournal* 80 (2015): 637–652, https://doi.org/10.1007/s10708-014-9568-4; Ian T. Ruginski, Sarah H. Creem-Regehr, Jeanine K. Stefanucci, and Elizabeth Cashdan, "GPS Use Negatively Affects Environmental Learning through Spatial Transformation Abilities," *Journal of Environmental Psychology* 64 (2019): 12–20, https://doi.org/10.1016/j.jenvp.2019.05.001.

21. Brett Frischmann and Evan Selinger, *Re-Engineering Humanity* (Cambridge: Cambridge University Press, 2018), 95.

22. Interview with Sheena Iyengar.

23. K. L. Keller and R. Staelin, "Effects of Quality and Quantity of Information on Decision Effectiveness," *Journal of Consumer Research*, 14 (1987): 200–213, https://doi.org/10.1086/209106.

24. Martin Zwilling, "How Many More Online Dating Sites Do We Need?" *Forbes*, March 1, 2013.

Chapter 1

1. James Watson, *The Double Helix* (New York: Atheneum Press, 1968).

2. Walter Isaacson, *The Code Breaker: Jennifer Doudna, Gene Editing, and the Future of the Human Race*, 1st ed. (New York: Simon & Schuster, 2021); Alison Abbott, "The Quiet Revolutionary: How the Co-Discovery of CRISPR Explosively Changed Emmanuelle Charpentier's Life," *Nature,* April 28, 2016: https://api.semanticscholar.org/CorpusID:4449749.

3. A video of Doudna's Nobel Prize acceptance speech, given on December 8, 2020, is available at *The Noble Prize,* https://www.nobelprize.org/prizes/chemistry/2020/doudna/lecture/.

4. "Jennifer A. Doudna—Facts—2020," Nobel Prizes and Laureates, *The Nobel Prize,* 2020, https://www.nobelprize.org/prizes/chemistry/2020/doudna/facts/.

5. "Jennifer A. Doudna—Facts—2020," Nobel Prizes and Laureates, *The Nobel Prize,* 2020, https://www.nobelprize.org/prizes/chemistry/2020/doudna/facts/.

6. "WHO Launches Global Registry on Human Genome Editing," WHO news release, August 29, 2019, https://www.who.int/news/item/29-08-2019-who-launches-global-registry-on-human-genome-editing; M. Araki and T. Ishii, "International Regulatory Landscape and Integration of Corrective Genome Editing into In Vitro Fertilization," *Reproductive Biology and Endocrinology* 12, no. 108 (2014), https://doi.org/10.1186/1477-7827-12-108, source on 30 countries; E. S. Lander, F. Baylis, F. Zhang, E. Charpentier, P. Berg, et al, "Adopt a Moratorium on Heritable Genome Editing," *Nature,* March 13, 2019, https://www.nature.com/articles/d41586-019-00726-5.

7. Jennifer Doudna, "How CRISPR Lets Us Edit Our DNA," TEDGlobal, London, October 20, 2015, https://www.ted.com/talks/jennifer_doudna_how_crispr_lets_us_edit_our_dna/transcript?language=en.

8. White House, Office of Science and Technology Policy, "Blueprint for an AI Bill of Rights: Making Automated Systems Work for the American People," white paper, October 2022, https://www.whitehouse.gov/ostp/ai-bill-of-rights/what-is-the-blueprint-for-an-ai-bill-of-rights/.

9. European Commission, *Proposal for a Regulation of the European Parliament and of the Council: Laying Down Harmonised Rules on Artificial Intelligence (Artificial Intelligence Act) and Amending Certain Union Legislative Acts* (Brussels: EC, April 21, 2021).

10. See, for example, the Universal Guidelines for AI, developed by the Center for AI and Digital Policy (https://thepublicvoice.org/ai-universal-guidelines/), and the Institute of Electrical and Electronics Engineers (IEEE) Global Initiative on Ethics

of Autonomous and Intelligent Systems (https://standards
.ieee.org/industry-connections/ec/autonomous-systems/).

11. Interviews and correspondence with software engineers,
2018–2022.

12. Interview with Casey Cerretani, February/March 2018, and
correspondence, August 2022–February 2023.

13. Bianca Bosker, "The Binge Breaker," *The Atlantic*, November
2016, https://www.theatlantic.com/magazine/archive/2016/11
/the-binge-breaker/501122/; Casey Newton, "Google's New Focus on Well-Being Started Five Years Ago with this Presentation," *The Verge*, May 10, 2018, https://www.theverge.com
/2018/5/10/17333574/google-android-p-update-tristan-harris
-design-ethics; Center for Humane Technology website, https://
www.humanetech.com/; Tristan Harris and Aza Raskin, *Your
Undivided Attention* podcast series, https://www.tristanharris
.com/#podcast.

14. Mohar Chatterjee, "5 Questions for Cathy O'Neil," *Politico*,
September 9, 2022, https://www.politico.com/newsletters
/digital-future-daily/2022/09/09/5-questions-for-cathy-oneil
-00055944.

15. "The Signals Network | Whistleblower Support Organization,"
accessed January 25, 2023, https://thesignalsnetwork.org/.

16. Interview with Casey Cerretani.

17. Howard Rheingold, *The Virtual Community* (Reading, MA:
Addison-Wesley, 1993), 7.

Chapter 2

1. Anastasiya Lebedev, "The Man Who Saved the World Fi-
nally Recognized," MosNews/Association of World Citizens,
May 21, 2004: David Hoffman, "I Had a Funny Feeling in
My Gut," *Washington Post*, February 12, 1999, https://www

.washingtonpost.com/wp-srv/inatl/longterm/coldwar/soviet
10.htm.

2. Branka Marijan, "The Case for the Petrov Rule," *The Plough-
shares Monitor* 38, no. 4 (Winter 2017).

3. Seth Baum, "Tackling Near and Far AI Threats at Once," Bulletin of Atomic Scientists, October 6, 2016.

4. Email correspondence. Marka Szabolcs is Walter O. Le-
Croy, Jr. Professor of Physics at Columbia University in New
York. He was Juliette's physics professor there in 2021. He
was kind enough to respond to her email inquiry for this
book in September 2022.

5. Daisuke Wakabayashi, "Self-Driving Uber Car Kills Pedestrian
in Arizona, Where Robots Roam," *New York Times*, March 19,
2018, https://www.nytimes.com/2018/03/19/technology/uber
-driverless-fatality.html; "Uber Self-Driving Crash: Footage
Shows Moment before Impact," *BBC News*, March 22, 2018,
https://www.bbc.com/news/world-us-canada-43497364.

6. Ron S. Dembo, *Risk Thinking in an Uncertain World* (Bloom-
ington, IN: Archway Books, 2021), chap. 7.

7. Carolyn Said, "Uber Puts the Brakes on Testing Robot Cars in
California after Arizona Fatality," *San Francisco Chronicle,*
March 27, 2018, https://www.sfchronicle.com/business/article
/Uber-pulls-out-of-all-self-driving-car-testing-in-12785490
.php; Andrew J. Hawkins, "Uber's Self-Driving Cars Return to
Public Roads For The First Time Since Fatal Crash," *The Verge,*
https://www.theverge.com/2018/12/20/18148946/uber-self
-driving-car-return-public-road-pittsburgh-crash.

8. R. Parasuraman and D. Manzey, "Complacency and Bias in
Human Use of Automation: An Attentional Integration," *The
Journal of the Human Factors and Ergonomics Society*, June
2010, 52no. 3 (June 2010): 381–410; National Transportation

Safety Board, "Collision Between Vehicle Controlled by Developmental Automated Driving System and Pedestrian," November 19, 2019, https://www.ntsb.gov/news/events/Pages/2019-HWY18MH010-BMG.aspx; A.R. Wagner, J. Borenstein and A. Howard, "Overtrust in the Robotic Age," *Communications of the ACM*, 61, no. 9 (Sept. 2018): 22,: link.gale.com/apps/doc/A552775279/ITOF?u=nysl_me_newyorku&sid=bookmark-ITOF&xid=f01d1379.

9. Lauren Smiley, "'I'm the Operator': The Aftermath of a Self-Driving Tragedy," *Wired*, March 8, 2022, https://www.wired.com/story/uber-self-driving-car-fatal-crash/; Vivek Haldar, "Uber Self-Driving Car Crash: The Role of Automation Complacency," *YouTube*, November 25, 2019, https://www.youtube.com/watch?v=_lK3PXgfrGI.

10. "Butterflies, Tornadoes, and Time Travel," *APS (Advancing Physics) News* 13, no. 4 (June 2004), https://www.aps.org/publications/apsnews/200406/butterfly-effect.cfm.

11. Dembo, *Risk Thinking*, chap. 2.

12. Audrow Nash, "Solar Powered Robotic Weeding, with Helen Greiner," *Sense Think Act* podcast, March 22, 2022, https://www.sensethinkact.com/episodes/16-helen-greiner.

13. Nash, "Solar Powered Robotic Weeding, with Helen Greiner."

14. Kyle Wiggers, "Sweeping Changes: How iRobot Evolved from Military Robots to Autonomous Vacuums," *VentureBeat*, June 18, 2019, https://venturebeat.com/business/sweeping-changes-how-irobot-evolved-from-military-robots-to-autonomous-vacuums/.

15. Gideon Rose, "She, Robot: A Conversation with Helen Greiner," *Foreign Affairs*, January–February 2015, https://www.foreignaffairs.com/interviews/2014-12-08/she-robot. See also Darren D'Addario, "If Robots Happen to Make Things

More Efficient, You Want to Be the Place That Has Them," *Afflictor.com*, December 15, 2014, https://afflictor.com/2014/12/15/if-robots-happen-to-make-things-more-efficient-you-want-to-be-the-place-that-has-them/.

16. Interview with Lynn Cherny, Jan-Feb 2018, and correspondence, Oct-Dec 2022. For more information about her, see www.ghostweather.com.

17. Interview with Lynn Cherny.

18. Interview with Casey Cerretani.

19. Jeff Orlowski, *The Social Dilemma*, Netflix, 2020; "Protecting Kids Online: Testimony from a Facebook Whistleblower," US Senate Committee on Commerce, Science & Transportation, subcommittee hearing with Frances Haugen, October 5, 2021; https://www.commerce.senate.gov/2021/10/protecting%20kids%20online:%20testimony%20from%20a%20facebook%20whistleblower.

20. This EU AIA background document explicitly names the TikTok feature which targets videos based on what people already watch: Andrea Renda, Jane Arroyo, Rosanna Fanni, Moritz Laurer, Agnes Sipiczki, Timothy Yeung (CEPS), George Maridis, Meena Fernandes, Gabor Endrodi, Simona Milio (ICF), Vivien Devenyi, Stefan Georgiev, and Ghislain de Pierrefeu (Wavestone), Study to Support an Impact Assessment of Regulatory Requirements for Artificial Intelligence in Europe, Final Report (D5), Contract number LC-01528103, European Commission, 2021, page 31ff.

21. Sara Morrison and Shirin Ghaffary, "Meta Hasn't 'Really Learned the Right Lesson,' Whistleblower Frances Haugen Says," *Business Insider*, September 6, 2022, https://www.vox.com/recode/2022/9/6/23333517/frances-haugen-code-meta-facebook-whistleblower.

22. Scott Pelley, "Whistleblower: Facebook is Misleading the Public on Progress Against Hate Speech, Violence, Misinformation," *CBS News 60 Minutes*, October 4, 2021.

23. Marcy Gordon and Barbara Ortutay, "'The Buck Stops with Mark': Ex-Facebook Manager Criticizes Zuckerberg, Calls for Oversight," *CBS8*, October 5, 2021; "Protecting Kids Online," Frances Haugen testimony.

24. Interview with Marc Rotenberg, founder for the Center of AI and Digital Policy; Interview with Daniel Lim, Salesforce .com and World Economic Forum; Kay Firth-Butterfield, Karen Silverman and Benjamin Larsen, "Understanding the US 'AI Bill of Rights'—and How It Can Help Keep AI Accountable," *World Economic Forum*, October 14, 2022, https://www.weforum.org/agenda/2022/10/understanding-the-ai-bill-of-rights-protection/; Richard Vanderford, "New York's Landmark AI Bias Law Prompts Uncertainty," *Wall Street Journal,* September 21, 2022, https://www.wsj.com/articles/new-yorks-landmark-ai-bias-law-prompts-uncertainty-11663752602#:~:text=A%20New%20York%20City%20law,can%20face%20fines%E2%80%94for%20violations.

25. "Wyden, Booker and Clarke Introduce Algorithmic Accountability Act of 2022 to Require New Transparency and Accountability For Automated Decision Systems," press release, Office of Ron Wyden, February 3, 2022.

26. Future of Life Institute, *The AI Act: Analyses,* web page, https://artificialintelligenceact.eu/analyses/; on most comprehensive: Edwards, L. (2022), Regulating AI in Europe: Four Problems and Four Solutions. Ada Lovelace Institute, https://www.adalovelaceinstitute.org/report/regulatingai-in-europe/.

27. Mauritz Kop, "The Pyramid of Criticality for AI Systems," in "EU Artificial Intelligence Act: The European Approach

to AI," *Transatlantic Antitrust and IPR Developments,*2021, https://law.stanford.edu/publications/eu-artificial-intelligence -act-the-european-approach-to-ai/; https://digital-strategy.ec .europa.eu/en/policies/regulatory-framework-ai. Correspondence with Mauritz Kop.

28. European Commission, Proposal for a Regulation of the European Parliament and of the Council, Laying Down Harmonised Rules on Artificial Intelligence (Artificial Intelligence Act) and Amending Certain Union Legislative Acts, Explanatory Memorandum, April 21, 2021, page 5; Mark MacCarthy, Kenneth Propp, "Machines Learn That Brussels Writes the Rules: The EU's New AI Regulation," *Lawfare,* April 28, 2021; Melissa Heikkilä, "6 Key Battles Ahead For Europe's AI Law," *Politico,* April 21, 2021.

29. Email correspondence with Ryan Carrier; Council of the European Union, Memorandum 13955/22, Interinstitutional File: 2021/0106(COD), November 3, 2022; Natasha Lomas, "Europe's AI Act Contains Powers to Order AI Models Destroyed or Retrained, Says Legal Expert," *TechCrunch,* April 1, 2022, https://techcrunch.com/2022/04/01/ai-act-powers/.

30. Interview with Ryan Carrier, August 2022; and correspondence, October 2022–January 2023.

31. Lilian Edwards, "Regulating AI in Europe: Four Problems and Four Solutions," *Ada Lovelace Institute, 2022,* https:// www.adalovelaceinstitute.org/report/regulatingai-in -europe/.

32. European Commission, "Proposal for a Regulation of the European Parliament and of the Council, Laying Down Harmonised Rules on Artificial Intelligence (Artificial Intelligence Act) and Amending Certain Union Legislative Acts, Explanatory Memorandum," April 21, 2021, section 11, page 10; email correspondence with Daniel Lim, January

2023; Benjamin Cedric Larsen, "The Geopolitics of AI and The Rise of Digital Sovereignty," *Brookings Institution,* December 8, 2022, https://www.brookings.edu/research/the -geopolitics-of-ai-and-the-rise-of-digital-sovereignty/.

Chapter 3

1. The Boeing story came from several sources: Joseph Rhee, Gerry Wagschal, and Jinsol Jung, "How Boeing 737 MAX's Flawed Flight Control System Led to 2 Crashes That Killed 346," *ABCNews,* November 27, 2020, https://abcnews.go.com /US/boeing-737-maxs-flawed-flight-control-system-led/story ?id=74321424; Dominic Gates, "Citing Safety Concerns, Whistleblowers Urge Revamp of Aging Boeing 737 MAX Cockpit," *Seattle Times,* April 19, 2022; Andy Pasztor, Andrew Tangel, Robert Wall, and Alison Side, "How Boeing's 737 MAX Failed," *Wall Street Journal,* March 27, 2019, https://www.wsj.com/articles/how-boeings-737-max-failed -11553699239; Michael Laris, Lori Aratani, and Ashley Halsey III, "FAA Chief Says Pilot Decisions Contributed to Boeing 737 Max Crashes," *Washington Post,* May 15, 2019, https://www.washingtonpost.com/transportation/2019/05 /15/faa-chief-be-pressed-boeing-max-while-would-be -replacement-faces-questions-his-approach-air-safety/; and Rory Kennedy, dir., *Downfall: The Case against Boeing,* Netflix, February 18, 2022.

2. European Commission, "Proposal for a Regulation of the European Parliament and of the Council, Laying Down Harmonised Rules on Artificial Intelligence (Artificial Intelligence Act) and Amending Certain Union Legislative Acts, Explanatory Memorandum," section 11 (April 21, 2021): 10; email correspondence with Daniel Lim, Janu-

ary 2023; Benjamin Cedric Larsen, "The Geopolitics of AI and The Rise of Digital Sovereignty," *Brookings Institution,* December 8, 2022, https://www.brookings.edu/research/the -geopolitics-of-ai-and-the-rise-of-digital-sovereignty/.

3. Interview with Anand Rao, July 2022, and correspondence, November 2022.

4. Diane Vaughan, "The Dark Side of Organizations: Mistake, Misconduct and Disaster," *Annual Review of Sociology* 25 (1999): 271–305.

5. Kimberly D. Krawiec, "Cosmetic Compliance and the Failure of Negotiated Governance," Washington *University Law Quarterly* 81, no. 2 (2003): 487–544, https://scholarship.law .duke.edu/faculty_scholarship/2046.

6. Lauren Kaori Gurley, "Internal Documents Show Amazon's Dystopian System for Tracking Workers Every Minute of Their Shifts," *Vice Motherboard,* June 2, 2022, https://www.vice.com /en/article/5dgn73/internal-documents-show-amazons -dystopian-system-for-tracking-workers-every-minute-of-their -shifts; "The Amazon Labor Union Took on America's Most Powerful Company—and Won," *Vice Motherboard,* April 4, 2022, https://www.vice.com/en/article/bvnkxa/the-amazon -labor-union-took-on-the-worlds-richest-manand-won.

7. Jodi Kantor and Arya Sundaram, "The Rise of the Worker Productivity Score," *New York Times,* August 14, 2022, https:// www.nytimes.com/interactive/2022/08/14/business/worker -productivity-tracking.html.

8. Interview with Casey Cerretani.

9. J. White, A. Bandura, and L. Bero, "Moral Disengagement in the Corporate World," *Accountability in Research* 16 (2009): 41–74. Also see Albert Bandura, *Moral Disengagement: How People Do Harm and Live with Themselves* (New York: Worth Publishers, 2015).

10. Cathy O'Neil, *Weapons of Math Destruction: How Big Data Increases Inequality and Threatens Democracy* (New York: Crown, 2016), 8, 29.

11. "History of the OSI," *Open Source Initiative*, October 2018, https://opensource.org/history; "History of Wikipedia," *Wikipedia*, December 2022, https://en.wikipedia.org/wiki/History _of_Wikipedia#; Freshlight Money, "The History of Quora," *Vocal*, December 2022, https://vocal.media/futurism/the -history-of-quora-s7gmr10v3z; Steven Levy, *Hackers: Heroes of the Computer Revolution* (New York: Doubleday, 1984); John Markoff, *What the Dormouse Said: How the Sixties Counterculture Shaped the Personal Computer Industry* (New York: Viking Press, 2005).

12. D. Gunning, E. Vorm, J. Y. Wang, and M. Turek, "DARPA's Explainable AI (XAI) Program: A Retrospective," *Applied AI Letters* 2 (2021): e61, https://doi.org/10.1002/ail2.61.

13. This point was made during a July 20, 2022, live question-and-answer session about XAI on LinkedIn, moderated by Ansgar Koene, professor at the University of Nottingham and working group chair for IEEE's Standard on Algorithm Bias Consideration.

14. Interview with Tymon Mattoszko, Jan–Feb 2018, and correspondence, Jan 2018–February 2023.

15. C. Metz, "In Two Moves, AlphaGo and Lee Sedol Redefined the Future," *Wired*, March 16, 2016, https://www.wired.com /2016/03/two-moves-alphago-lee-sedol-redefined-future/.

16. Iyad Rahwan, Jacob W. Crandall, and Jean-François Bonnefon, "Intelligent Machines as Social Catalysts," *Proceedings of the National Academy of Sciences (PNAS)* 117, no. 14 (April 7, 2020): 7555–7557, https://doi.org/10.1073/pnas .2002744117; Luca Pion-Tonachini, Kristofer Bouchard, et al, "Learning from Learning Machines: A New Generation of

AI Technology to Meet the Needs of Science," *DeepAI*, November 27, 2021, https://deepai.org/publication/learning-from-learning-machines-a-new-generation-of-ai-technology-to-meet-the-needs-of-science.

17. Tom Simonite, "Google's AI Guru Wants Computers to Think More Like Brains," *Wired*, December 12, 2018, https://www.wired.com/story/googles-ai-guru-computers-think-more-like-brains/.

18. Ralph Richard Banks, "Why More Black Women Should Consider Marrying White Men," *New York Post*, April 1, 2022.

19. Interview with David Bankston, June 2022.

20. Ryan Jones, "What Is a Google Broad Core Algorithm Update?" *Search Engine Journal*, January 23, 2022, https://www.searchenginejournal.com/what-is-a-google-broad-core-algorithm-update/264261/.

21. For example, see Timnit Gebru, Jamie Morgenstern, Briana Vecchione, Jennifer Wortman Vaughan, Hanna Wallach, Hal Daumé III, and Kate Crawford, "Datasheets for Datasets," *Communications of the ACM* 64, no. 12 (December 2021): 86–92, https://doi 10.1145/3458723. Also see Inioluwa Deborah Raji, Andrew Smart, Rebecca N. White, Margaret Mitchell, Timnit Gebru, Ben Hutchinson, Jamila Smith-Loud, Daniel Theron, and Parker Barnes, "Closing the AI Accountability Gap: Defining an End-to-End Framework for Internal Algorithmic Auditing," *arXiv* (2020), https://arxiv.org/abs/2001.00973. Another source is Kush R. Varshney, *Trustworthy Machine Learning* (self-pub., 2022), http://www.trustworthymachinelearning.com. Data audit organizations whose leaders we talked to include O'Neil Risk Consulting & Algorithmic Auditing (www.orcaarisk.com) and ForHumanity (www.forhumanity.center).

22. Email exchange with Marka Szabolcs, September–December 2022.
23. Interview with Alan Morrison, May 2022, and correspondence, October 2022–January 2023.

Chapter 4

1. Insight from an interview with Michael Rosenbaum, founder of Catalyte and Arena, August 2022; and correspondence, September 2022–January 2023. Disclosure: Art first learned about this story as a paid contract editor on a project with Rosenbaum and Arena in 2020.
2. Interview with Catherine Booker, November 14, 2022, and correspondence, December 2022–January 2023.
3. Interview with Michael Rosenbaum.
4. Opportunity@Work, "Spotlight on Black Stars," 2022, https://opportunityatwork.org/our-solutions/stars-insights/blackstars/black-stars-download/.
5. Tim Newcomb, "Amira Literacy Uses Artificial Intelligence to Analyze and Support K-3 Students' Reading Skills, Opens Up Greater At-Home Learning Options," *The 74*, February 8, 2021, https://www.the74million.org/article/amira-literacy-uses-artificial-intelligence-to-analyze-and-support-k-3-students-reading-skills-opens-up-greater-at-home-learning-options/.
6. Interview with Michael Rosenbaum.
7. An evocative documentary on this theme is Sandy Smolan, dir., *The Human Face of Big Data*, WMHT, February 24, 2016, https://vimeo.com/152311763/description.
8. Arvind Narayanan and Vitaly Shmatikov, "How to Break Anonymity of the Netflix Prize Dataset," Cornell University Open Archive, *arXiv* (2006), https://doi.org/10.48550/arxiv.cs/0610105.

9. Email exchange with John Battelle, October–November 2022. Battelle, a senior research scholar at Columbia University School of International and Public Affairs (SIPA) and co-founder and CEO of Recount Media, worked with four student researchers (Zoe Martin, Natasha Bhuta, Matthew Albasi, and Veronica Penney) to produce a presentation on mapping data flows. See Columbia SIPA, "Mapping Data: How the Largest Tech Firms Use Your Data," *YouTube*, video, 47:36, November 19, 2019, https://www.youtube.com/watch?v=b5H9tUSqnas.

10. Nicole Wetsman, "Mental Health Apps Have Terrible Privacy Protections," *The Verge*, May 2, 2022, https://www.theverge.com/2022/5/2/23045250/mozilla-mental-health-app-privacy-analysis.

11. Jordan Parker Erb, "Mozilla Slaps 18 Period and Pregnancy Tracking Apps and Devices with a 'Privacy Not Included' Warning Label," *Insider*, August 17, 2022, https://www.businessinsider.com/mozilla-period-pregnancy-apps-privacy-warning-label-flo-glow-ovia-2022-8; Nicole Wetsman, "Period and Pregnancy Tracking Apps Have Bad Privacy Protections, Report Finds," *The Verge*, August 17, 2022, https://www.theverge.com/2022/8/17/23306570/period-tracking-apps-privacy; Wetsman, "Mental Health Apps Have Terrible Privacy Protections."

12. Shoshana Zuboff, *The Age of Surveillance Capitalism* (New York: Hachette/Public Affairs, 2019), chap. 1.

13. Heather Zeiger, "Surveillance and Silence at the 2022 Beijing Winter Olympics," *Mind Matters News*, February 3, 2022, https://mindmatters.ai/2022/02/surveillance-and-silence-at-the-2022-beijing-winter-olympics/.

14. Jamie Tarabay and Sarah Zheng, "Olympic Athletes Advised to Leave Phones at Home to Dodge Spying," Bloomberg, January

17, 2022, https://www.bloomberg.com/news/articles/2022-01 -17/olympic-athletes-told-to-leave-phones-at-home-to-dodge -spying.

15. Eileen Guo, "A Roomba Recorded a Woman On the Toilet. How Did Screenshots End Up On Facebook?," *MIT Technology Review,* December 19, 2022, https://www.technologyreview .com/2022/12/19/1065306/roomba-irobot-robot-vacuums -artificial-intelligence-training-data-privacy/; Eileen Guo, "Roomba Testers Feel Misled After Intimate Images Ended Up On Facebook," *MIT Technology Review,* January 10, 2023, https://www.technologyreview.com/2023/01/10/1066500 /roomba-irobot-robot-vacuum-beta-product-testers-consent -agreement-misled/.

16. Khari Johnson, "Iran Says Face Recognition Will ID Women Breaking Hijab Laws," *Wired,* January 10, 2023, https://www .wired.com/story/iran-says-face-recognition-will-id-women -breaking-hijab-laws/?mc_cid=476a7f16e9&mc_eid=4aaf0 b1e20.

17. Antonio Regalado and Jessica Leber, "Intel Fuels a Rebellion around Your Data," *MIT Technology Review,* May 20, 2013, https://www.technologyreview.com/2013/05/20/178389 /intel-fuels-a-rebellion-around-your-data/.

18. WeTheData, "John Perry Barlow: Your Personal Data—Who Owns and Controls It?" *YouTube,* video, 2:05, October 4, 2012, https://www.youtube.com/watch?v=-JLLGKt2QmA.

19. WeTheData, "Bill Joy on the Pros and Cons of Being Clever with Vibrant Data," *YouTube,* video, 2:22, November 11, 2012, https://www.youtube.com/watch?v=QiPUkAcXD5o&t =6s; WeTheData.

20. WeTheData, "The Personal Data Economy—Simplicity on the Other Side of Complexity, *YouTube,* video, 2:47, February 15, 2013, https://www.youtube.com/watch?v=GOgUAwLL2zg.

21. Wouter H. Dessein and Juliette Powell, "Setting Strategy at S Group: Finland's Largest Retailer Anticipates Amazon's Arrival," Case No. CCW190305, Columbia CaseWorks, Columbia Business School, April 16, 2020, https://www.thecasecentre.org/products/view?id=163001

22. Emily Steel, Callum Locke, Emily Cadman, and Ben Freese, "How Much Is Your Personal Data Worth?" *Financial Times*, June 12, 2013, https://ig.ft.com/how-much-is-your-personal-data-worth/#axzz2z2agBB6R. Also see Paulius Jurcys, "What Is the Value of Your Data?" *Medium*, September 5, 2019, https://towardsdatascience.com/what-is-the-value-of-your-data-9341cd019b4d.

23. Adam Satariano, "Meta's Ad Practices Ruled Illegal Under E.U. Law," *New York Times*, January 4, 2023, https://www.nytimes.com/2023/01/04/technology/meta-facebook-eu-gdpr.html; Natasha Lomas, "Meta Dodged a €4BN Privacy Fine Over Unlawful Ads, Argues GDPR Complainant," *TechCrunch*, January 19, 2023, https://techcrunch.com/2023/01/19/meta-ads-noyb-epdb-gdpr-complaint/.

24. "MobileCoin CEO Joshua Goldbard Featured on Coindesk TV's 'The Hash,'" MobileCoin (blog), September 22, 2021, https://developers.mobilecoin.com/blog/mobilecoin-ceo-joshua-goldbard-featured-on-coindesk-tvs-the-hash.

25. Interview with Sean Gayle, July–August 2022.

26. Interview with Casey Cerretani.

27. Jaron Lanier and E. Glen Weyl, "A Blueprint for a Better Digital Society," *Harvard Business Review*, September 26, 2018, https://hbr.org/2018/09/a-blueprint-for-a-better-digital-society; Imanol Arrieta-Ibarra, Leonard Goff, Diego Jiménez-Hernández, Jaron Lanier, and E. Glen Weyl, "Should We Treat Data as Labor? Moving beyond 'Free,'" *AEA Papers and Proceedings*, vol. 108 (2018): 38–42, https://doi.org/10.1257/pandp.20181003.

28. Interview with Anand Rao.

29. Juliette Powell, unpublished research, Columbia University, 2018.

Chapter 5

1. Interview with Sean Gayle, July–August 2022.

2. Vedran Omanović and Ann Langley, "Assimilation, Integration or Inclusion? A Dialectical Perspective on the Organizational Socialization of Migrants," *Journal of Management Inquiry,* 32 no. 1 (December 13, 2021): 76–97, https://doi.org/10.1177/10564926211063777; Roula Amire, "Well-being Study: 1 Out of 6 U.S. Employees Flourishing at Work," *Great Place to Work,* April 11, 2022, https://www.greatplacetowork.com/resources/blog/well-being-study-1-out-of-6-u-s-employees-flourishing-at-work; Lacee Jacobs, Mac Quartarone, and Kate Hemingway, "Do Your Diversity Initiatives Promote Assimilation Over Inclusion?," *Harvard Business Review,* February 2, 2022, https://hbr.org/2022/02/do-your-diversity-initiatives-promote-assimilation-over-inclusion.

3. Steve Lohr, "Facial Recognition Is Accurate, If You're a White Guy," *New York Times,* February 9, 2018, https://www.nytimes.com/2018/02/09/technology/facial-recognition-race-artificial-intelligence.html.

4. Joy Buolamwini, "Facing the Coded Gaze with Evocative Audits and Algorithmic Audits" (PhD thesis, MIT, 2022), 2022, hdl:1721.1/143396.

5. Joy Buolamwini and Timnit Gebru, "Gender Shades: Intersectional Accuracy Disparities in Commercial Gender Classification," *Proceedings of Machine Learning Research* 81 (2018): 1–15, http://proceedings.mlr.press/v81/buolamwini18a/buo

lamwini18a.pdf. See also Rachel Thomas, "The Far-Reaching Impact of Dr. Timnit Gebru," *The Gradient*, December 9, 2020, https://thegradient.pub/the-far-reaching-impacts-of-timnit-gebru/.

6. Buolamwini and Gebru, "Gender Shades."

7. Davide Castelvecchi, "Is Facial Recognition Too Biased to Be Let Loose?" *Nature*, November 18, 2020, https://www.nature.com/articles/d41586-020-03186-4.

8. Interview with Kevin Clark, December 2022, and correspondence, December 2022–February 2023.

9. Interview with Sean Gayle.

10. Interview with Cathy O'Neil, July 2022.

11. Interview with Casey Cerretani.

12. See the interview with Joy Buolamwini by Ian Tucker, "'A White Mask Worked Better': Why Algorithms Are Not Colour Blind," *The Guardian*, May 28, 2017, https://www.theguardian.com/technology/2017/may/28/joy-buolamwini-when-algorithms-are-racist-facial-recognition-bias.

13. David Stark with Daniel Beunza, Monique Girard, and János Lukács, *The Sense of Dissonance: Accounts of Worth in Economic Life* (Princeton, NJ: Princeton University Press, 2009), 184.

14. Nora Bateson, "Warm Data: Contextual Research and New Forms of Information," *Medium*, May 28, 2017, https://medium.com/hackernoon/warm-data-9f0fcd2a828c.

15. Jennifer Yales, EdD, "Humanizing the Data: A Path to More Compassionate Systems in Education Starting from the Inside Out," *Center for Systems Awareness: Stories from the Field*, Spring 2022, https://systemsawareness.org/stories-from-the-field-warming-the-data/.

Chapter 6

1. Zach Whittaker, "Clearview A.I. Ruled 'Illegal' by Canadian Privacy Authorities," *TechCrunch,* February 3, 2021, https:techcrunch.com/2021/02/03/clearview-ai-ruled-illegal -by-canadian-privacy-authorities/.

2. Interview with Peter Sloly, July 2022, and correspondence, October–November 2022.

3. Drew Harwell, "Clearview A.I. to Stop Selling Facial Recognition Tool to Private Firms," *Washington Post,* May 9, 2022, https:www.washingtonpost.com/technology/2022/05/09 /clearview-illinois-court-settlement/; Adam Schwartz, "Victory! More Lawsuits Appear Against Clearview's Face Surveillance," *Electronic Frontier Foundation,* February 2022, https: www.eff.org/deeplinks/2022/02/victory-another-law suit-proceeds-against-clearviews-face-surveillance.

4. Jan Kleinnijenhuis, "Who Knew What in the Allowance Affair? The Tangle of Protagonists Untangled," [in Dutch] *Trouw,* November 14, 2020, https://www.trouw.nl/politiek/wie-wist -wat-in-de-toeslagenaffaire-de-kluwen-van-hoofdrolspelers -ontward~b721c834/?referrer=https%3A%2F%2Fen .wikipedia.org%2F&utm_source=link&utm_medium =social&utm_campaign=shared_earned.

5. Ibid.

6. Christine Moser, Frank den Hond, and Dirk Lindebaum, "What Humans Lose When We Let AI Decide," *MIT Sloan Management Review,* February 7, 2022, https://sloanreview .mit.edu/article/what-humans-lose-when-we-let-ai-decide/.

7. "Dutch Childcare Benefit Scandal an Urgent Wake-Up Call to Ban Racist Algorithms," *Amnesty International,* October 25, 2021, https://www.amnesty.org/en/latest/news/2021 /10/xenophobic-machines-dutch-child-benefit-scandal/.

8. Kleinnijenhuis, "Who Knew What in the Allowance Affair?"

9. Interview with Christine Moser, June 2022, and correspondence, October 2022.

10. Thomas McBrien, Ben Winters, Enid Zhou, and Virginia Eubanks, "Screened and Scored in the District of Columbia," Electronic Privacy Information Center, 2022, https://epic.org/wp-content/uploads/2022/11/EPIC-Screened-in-DC-Report.pdf.

11. Stephanie Wykstra, "Government's Use of Algorithm Serves Up False Fraud Charges," *Undark*, June 1, 2020, https://undark.org/2020/06/01/michigan-unemployment-fraud-algorithm/.

12. Interview with Peter Sloly, July 2022, and correspondence, October–November 2022.

13. Interview with Marc Rotenberg, June 2022, and correspondence, November 2022–January 2023.

14. Interview with Alan Morrison.

15. Noam Scheiber and Kate Conger, "The Great Google Revolt," *New York Times*, February 18, 2020, https://www.nytimes.com/interactive/2020/02/18/magazine/google-revolt.html.

16. Email correspondence with Kevin Clark, December 2022.

17. Cameron Bird, Sean Captain, Elise Craig, Haley Cohen Gilliland, and Joy Shan, "The Tech Revolt," *California Sunday,* January 23, 2019, https://story.californiasunday.com/tech-revolt/.

18. Rick Levine, Christopher Locke, Doc Searls, and David Weinberger, *The Cluetrain Manifesto: The End of Business as Usual,* (New York: Basic Books, 2009); Berkman Klein Center for Internet & Society, https://cyber.harvard.edu/; Interview with Doc Searls, February–March 2018.

19. Interview with Doc Searls, February–March 2018.

20. Interview with Casey Cerretani.

21. Algorithmic Justice League, "Learn More," 2022, https://www.ajl.org/learn-more.

22. Diane Vaughan, "The Dark Side of Organizations: Mistake, Misconduct and Disaster," *Annual Review of Sociology* 25 (1999): 271–305; James O'Toole, *The Enlightened Capitalists: Cautionary Tales of Business Pioneers Who Tried to Do Well by Doing Good* (New York: HarperBusiness, 2019).

23. Interview with Casey Cerretani.

24. Interview with Cathy O'Neil.

25. Ansgar Koene, "Algorithmic Bias: Addressing Growing Concerns," *IEEE Technology and Society Magazine*, vol. 36, no. 2, June 2017, https://ieeexplore.ieee.org/document/7947257

26. Anand Rao, "Democratizing Artificial Intelligence Is a Double-Edged Sword," *Strategy+Business*, June 15, 2020, https://www.strategy-business.com/article/Democratizing-artificial-intelligence-is-a-double-edged-sword; and interview and email correspondence with Anand Rao.

27. Kimberly Kindy, "Insurers Force Change on Police Departments Long Resistant to It," *Washington Post*, September 14, 2022, https://www.washingtonpost.com/investigations/interactive/2022/police-misconduct-insurance-settlements-reform/.

28. Ibid.

Chapter 7

1. Charles Perrow, *Normal Accidents* (New York: Basic Books, 1984; 2d ed., Princeton, NJ: Princeton University Press, 1999). Also see Charles Perrow, "The Organizational Context of Human Factors Engineering," *Administrative Science Quarterly* 28 (1983): 521–541; Charles Perrow, *Complex Organ-*

izations, 3rd ed. (New York: Random House, 1986); Charles Perrow and Mauro F. Guillen, *The AIDS Disaster* (New Haven, CT: Yale University Press, 1990); Charles Perrow, "A Society of Organizations," *Theory & Society* 20 (1991): 763–794.

2. Diane Vaughan, *The Challenger Launch Decision: Risky Technology, Culture, and Deviance at NASA*, Enlarged ed. (Chicago: University of Chicago Press, 2016), page 8.

3. Vaughan, *The Challenger Launch Decision*, page 10.

4. Vaughan, *The Challenger Launch Decision*, page 487 and 29.

5. Diane Vaughan, Testimony before the Columbia Accident Investigation Board, 23 April 2003.

6. Correspondence with Steve Crandall, September–November 2022.

7. Perrow, *Normal Accidents*.

8. Alan Chan, "Loss of Control: 'Normal Accidents' and AI Systems" (paper prepared for ICLR 2021 Workshop on Responsible AI, 2021), https://www.achan.ca/publication/iclr-rai-2021-ai-risks/iclr-rai-2021-ai-risks.pdf. Also, interview with Alan Chan, November 2022.

9. Arwa Mahdawi, "The $300M Flip Flop: How Real-Estate Site Zillow's Side Hustle Went Badly Wrong," *The Guardian*, November 4, 2021, https://www.theguardian.com/business/2021/nov/04/zillow-homes-buying-selling-flip-flop,

10. Interview with John Sviokla, August 2022.

11. Ed Catmull, "How Pixar Fosters Collective Creativity," *Harvard Business Review*, September 2008, https://hbr.org/2008/09/how-pixar-fosters-collective-creativity.

12. Art Kleiner and Juliette Powell, "Bran Ferren on the Art of Innovation," *Strategy+Business*, October 21, 2015, https://www.strategy-business.com/article/00381.

13. Interview with Steve Crandall.

Chapter 8

1. US Department of Education, "Carol M. White Physical Education Program description," *US Department of Education, Office of Elementary and Secondary Education*, CFDA Number: 84.215F, September 6, 2016, https://www2.ed.gov/programs/whitephysed/index.html.

2. Brett Frischmann and Evan Selinger, *Re-Engineering Humanity* (Cambridge: Cambridge University Press, 2018), 21.

3. "What Is Frictionless Customer Experience and Why Is It Important for Your Business?" *Kayako Insights Blog*, 2022, https://kayako.com/blog/what-is-frictionless-customer-experience/.

4. Art Kleiner, "The Problem of Virtuous Leadership: Interview With Adam Smith Scholar Ryan Patrick Hanley," Strategy +Business, December 6, 2017, https://www.strategy-business.com/article/The-Problem-of-Virtuous-Leadership; Ryan Hanley, editor, *Adam Smith: His Life, Thought, and Legacy* (Princeton: Princeton University Press, 2016).

5. Hannah Arendt, *The Human Condition, 2nd Edition, introduction by Margaret Canovan* (Chicago: University of Chicago Press, 1958, 1998), page 5; Jill Jensen, "Educating Without Banisters: Hannah Arendt on Thinking, Willing, and Judging," (dissertation, University of British Columbia, January 2020).

6. Geoff Colvin and Ryan Derousseau, "Jeff Bezos's War With Friction," *Fortune*, February 2, 2017, https://fortune.com/2017/02/02/jeff-bezoss-war-with-friction/; Roger Dooley, *Friction: The Untapped Force That Can Be Your Most Powerful Advantage* (New York: McGraw-Hill, 2019).

7. George Packer, "Change the World," *New Yorker*, May 20, 2013, https://www.newyorker.com/magazine/2013/05/27/change-the-world.

8. Vishnupriya Sengupta and Suvarchala Narayanan, "India's New Unicorns," *Strategy+Business,* October 21, 2019, https:// www.strategy-business.com/feature/Indias-new-unicorns.

9. Steve Krug, *Don't Make Me Think, Revisited: A Common Sense Approach to Web Usability,* 3rd ed. (New Riders/Pearson, 2014). The book was first published in 2000.

10. Robert Kanigel, *The One Best Way: Frederick Winslow Taylor and the Enigma of Efficiency* (New York: Viking, 1997), prologue.

11. Brett M. Frischmann and Susan Benesch, "Friction-In-Design Regulation as 21st Century Time, Place and Manner Restriction," *SSRN,* August 1, 2022, http://dx.doi.org/10.2139 /ssrn.4178647.

12. Astro Teller, "Tips for Unleashing Radical Creativity," *Medium,* February 12, 2020, https://medium.com/thexblog/tips -for-unleashing-radical-creativity-f4ba55602e17.

13. David Stark, *The Sense of Dissonance* (Princeton, NJ: Princeton University Press, 2009), 109.

14. Teller, "Tips for Unleashing Radical Creativity."

15. Dorothy Leonard and Susaan Straus, "Putting Your Company's Whole Brain to Work," *Harvard Business Review,* July– August 1997, https://hbr.org/1997/07/putting-your-companys -whole-brain-to-work.

16. Paul Genberg, "Embracing Creative Abrasion at Your Conflict-Averse Company," *Forbes,* January 21, 2022, https://www.for bes.com/sites/forbesbusinesscouncil/2022/01/21/embracing -creative-abrasion-at-your-conflict-averse-company/?sh =78f614132274.

17. Stark, *The Sense of Dissonance,* chap. 2.

18. Conversation between Juliette Powell and Danny Hillis, summer 2016.

19. Stark, *The Sense of Dissonance,* 111.

20. Avi Dan, "The Secret That Inspires Cirque du Soleil's Culture of Innovation: Creative Friction," *Forbes.com*, May 29, 2012, https://www.forbes.com/sites/avidan/2012/05/29/the-secret -that-inspires-cirque-du-soleils-culture-of-innovation -creative-friction/?sh=58e2efb845f9.

21. Frischmann and Selinger, *Re-engineering Humanity*, page 26.

22. Teller, "Tips for Unleashing Radical Creativity."

23. Amy C. Edmondson, *The Fearless Organization: Creating Psychological Safety in the Workplace for Learning, Innovation, and Growth* (Hoboken, NJ: Wiley, 2018).

24. Teller is quoted in Grant Russell, "Building a Learning Culture: Lessons from X, The Moonshot Factory," *LinkedIn*, June 21, 2021, https://www.linkedin.com/pulse/building -learning-culture-lessons-from-x-moonshot-factory-russell/.

25. Kalley Huang, "Alarmed by AI Chatbots, Universities Start Revamping How They Teach," *New York Times*, January 16, 2023, https://www.nytimes.com/2023/01/16/technology/chatgpt -artificial-intelligence-universities.html.

26. This is also known as "conflict monitoring." See David Badre and Anthony D. Wagner, "Selection, Integration, and Conflict Monitoring: Assessing the Nature and Generality of Prefrontal Cognitive Control Mechanisms," *Neuron* 41, no. 3 (2004): 473–487, https://doi.org/10.1016/S0896-6273(03)00851-1; D. Head, K. M. Kennedy, K. M. Rodrigue, and N. Raz, "Age Differences in Perseveration: Cognitive and Neuroanatomical Mediators of Performance on the Wisconsin Card Sorting Test," *Neuropsychologia* 47 (2009): 1200–1203; Z. Zhou, H. Zhu, C. Li, and J. Wang, "Internet Addictive Individuals Share Impulsivity and Executive Dysfunction with Alcohol-Dependent Patients," *Frontiers in Behavioral Neuroscience* 8 (2014): 288, https://doi.org/10.3389/fnbeh.2014.00288; E. Wegmann, S. M. Müller, O. Turel, and M. Brand, "Interac-

tions of Impulsivity, General Executive Functions, and Specific Inhibitory Control Explain Symptoms of Social-Networks-Use Disorder: An Experimental Study," *Scientific Reports* 10, no. 3866 (2020), https://doi.org/10.1038/s41598-020-60819-4.

27. Cameron Anderson and Adam D. Galinsky, "Power, Optimism, and Risk-Taking," *European Journal of Social Psychology*, July 17, 2006, https://doi.org/10.1002/ejsp.324; A. D. Galinsky, J. C. Magee, M. E. Inesi, and D. H. Gruenfeld, "Power and Perspectives Not Taken," *Psychological Science* 17, no. 12 (2006): 1068–1074, https://doi.org/10.1111/j.1467-9280.2006.01824.x; Leigh Plunkett Tost, Francesca Gino, and Richard P. Larrick, "Power, Competitiveness, and Advice Taking: Why the Powerful Don't Listen," *Organizational Behavior and Human Decision Processes* 117, no. 1 (2012): 53–65, https://doi.org/10.1016/j.obhdp.2011.10.001.

28. Quoted in Stark, *The Sense of Dissonance*, 13–15.

29. Interview with Janet Thompson at McCann Global Headquarters in New York, October 2022, and correspondence October 2022.

30. Josh A. Goldstein, Girish Sastry, Micah Musser, Renee DiResta, Matthew Gentzel, and Katerina Sedova, "Generative Language Models and Automated Influence Operations: Emerging Threats and Potential Mitigations," ArXiv:2301.04246 [Cs] (January 2023), https://arxiv.org/abs/2301.04246; Stanford Internet Observatory Report Summary, https://cyber.fsi.stanford.edu/io/news/forecasting-potential-misuses-language-models-disinformation-campaigns-and-how-reduce-risk.

31. Teller, "Tips for Unleashing Radical Creativity."

32. Renée Richardson Gosline, "Why AI Customer Journeys Need More Friction," *Harvard Business Review*, June 9, 2022, https://hbr.org/2022/06/why-ai-customer-journeys-need-more-friction.

Conclusion

1. Iyad Rahwan and Manuel Cebrian, "Machine Behavior Needs to Be an Academic Discipline," *Nautilus*, March 20, 2018, https://nautil.us/machine-behavior-needs-to-be-an-academic-discipline-237022/.

2. Email correspondence with Marka Szabolcs, September–December 2022.

3. Kevin Roose, "Bing (Yes, Bing) Just Made Search Interesting Again," *New York Times,* February 8, 2023, https://www.nytimes.com/2023/02/08/technology/microsoft-bing-openai-artificial-intelligence.html?searchResultPosition=9.

4. Eli Collins and Zoubin Ghahramani, "LaMDA: Our Breakthough Conversation Technology," *Google*, May 18, 2021, https://blog.google/technology/ai/lamda/.

5. Meta AI, Demonstration Site, "BlenderBot: A Conversational AI Alternative," Accessed February 13, 2023, https://blenderbot.ai/; Charlie Hancock, "Meta's AI Chatbot Repeats Election and Anti-Semitic Conspiracies," *Bloomberg*, August 8, 2022, https://www.bloomberg.com/news/articles/2022-08-08/meta-s-ai-chatbot-repeats-election-and-anti-semitic-conspiracies?leadSource=uverify%20wall; Jovi Umawing, "Now It's BlenderBot's Turn to Make Shocking, Inappropriate, and Untrue Remarks," *Malwarebytes Labs*, August 10, 2022, https://www.malwarebytes.com/blog/news/2022/08/its-now-blenderbots-turn-to-make-shocking-inappropriate-and-untrue-remarks; News Staff, "How Long Did It Take for Meta's New Chatbot to Start Spewing Misinformation?," *Government Technology*, August 15, 2022, https://www.govtech.com/question-of-the-day/how-long-did-it-take-for-metas-new-chatbot-to-start-spewing-misinformation.

6. Davey Alba, "OpenAI Chatbot Spits Out Biased Musings, Despite Guardrails," *Bloomberg*, December 8, 2022, https://www.bloomberg.com/news/newsletters/2022-12-08/chatgpt-open-ai-s-chatbot-is-spitting-out-biased-sexist-results.
7. Kieran Snyder, "We Asked ChatGPT to Write Performance Reviews and They Are Wildly Sexist (and Racist), *Fast Company,* February 3, 2023, https://www.fastcompany.com/90844066/chatgpt-write-performance-reviews-sexist-and-racist.
8. Iyad Rahwan, Manuel Cebrian, Nick Obradovich et al, "Machine Behaviour," *Nature* 568 (April 24, 2019): 477–486, https://doi.org/10.1038/s41586-019-1138-y.

Glossary

AI dilemma—The challenges of managing and regulating the rapidly-evolving group of Triple-A systems already embedded in everyday life, whose attributes make them both highly beneficial and highly dangerous. (Introduction)

algorithmic systems—Software products made up of algorithms, which are instructions for a computer to follow in order to execute a task or solve a problem. One of the three types of Triple-A systems. (Introduction)

Apex Benchmark—A model of the factors needed for evaluating self-regulation of Triple-A systems. (Chapter 6)

artificial intelligence (AI)—The theory and development of computer systems able to perform tasks that might otherwise require human intelligence, such as visual perception, speech recognition, decision making, and translation between languages. One of the three types of Triple-A systems. (Introduction)

Artificial Intelligence Act (AIA)—A proposed law for the European Union containing a comprehensive framework for AI risk that is likely to set the standard for worldwide regulation if it passes. (Chapter 1)

automated systems—A form of technology, software, or hardware designed to function with little to no human supervision or intervention. One of the three types of Triple-A systems. (Introduction)

automation complacency—The tendency of people to trust automated systems and not pay attention to them, even when charged with overseeing them. (Chapter 2)

autonomous vehicle (AV)—Also known as a "self-driving" vehicle, it is a vehicle capable of performing all the necessary functions of driving using sensors, cameras, and algorithms with little to no human involvement. (Introduction, Chapter 2)

behavioral surplus—Shoshana Zuboff's term for personal data that can be monetized as fuel for predictive algorithms, such as those used in targeted advertising. (Chapter 4)

bias—An ingrained preference, prejudice, or strong opinion toward or against specific people or things. Bias can be embedded in the data or design of a Triple-A system. (Chapter 5)

Big Tech—The group of the largest, most dominant technology companies in the industry. (Chapter 1)

black box—See "Closed Box." (Chapter 3)

calculus of intentional risk—A framework for estimating the trade-offs and uncertainties related to Triple-A systems to help decide how to proceed. (Conclusion)

chatbot—An algorithmic system designed to simulate conversation with humans, especially over the internet. (Conclusion)

closed box—An opaque system that does not foster trust and avoids scrutiny by obscuring how it functions. This term is replacing the previously used term "Black Box." (Chapter 3)

cold data—Nora Bateson's term for purely quantitative statistics that don't express a human context or underlying relationships. (Chapter 5)

confirmation bias—The tendency to pay more attention to data that reinforces an existing point of view. Triple-A systems are prone to confirmation bias. (Chapter 5)

conversational AI—A software category of technologies that produce human-like interactions through automated messaging and voice-enabled applications. (Conclusion)

corporate logic—The logic of ownership, markets, and growth. It prioritizes money, profit, expansion, new business, and dominance over competitors, often leading to decisions that favor expedience. (Chapter 1)

creative friction—Activity designed to disrupt heedless momentum. It often involves open, in-depth communication among people with diverse perspectives. (Chapter 8)

data ownership—Control over the use and monetization of your personal data so that every company that benefits from it must ask your permission. (Chapter 4)

deep learning—A part of a broader family of machine learning methods based on artificial neural networks with representation learning. Learning can be supervised, semi-supervised, or unsupervised. (Introduction)

engineering logic—The perspective of technologists. It prioritizes employers' interests, being a part of a highly-skilled community and contributing to challenging work. A self-selected few may prioritize the users affected by their work. (Chapter 1)

explainable AI (XAI)—Also known as transparent or open-source AI. These systems keep the logic and purpose of the software accessible to stakeholders affected by it so they can question and critique it when necessary. (Chapter 3)

four logics of power—Four main perspectives that influence artificial intelligence: engineering logic, corporate logic, social justice logic, and government logic. (Chapter 1)

frictionlessness—The aspirational state of minimal impediment, and an addictive attribute of Triple-A and other systems. (Chapter 8)

generative AI—The generic name for AI systems designed to create content and communicate directly with people, including chatbots and conversational AI. A wave of generative AI, including OpenAI's ChatGPT and DALL-E, was released starting in 2022 and was adopted with extreme speed. (Conclusion)

Gini coefficient—A statistical measurement of the distribution of income across a nation or social group in order to highlight income inequality. (Introduction)

government logic—The perspective of authority and security. It prioritizes protecting the nation from outside forces and providing support and public services to the citizens. (Chapter 1)

high-risk AI—Triple-A activity that could cause harm to people's health, safety, or fundamental rights but also provides significant value. According to EU AIA, it should be audited and highly regulated. (Chapter 2)

illusion of control—Ellen Langer's term for the misleading sensation of having agency over events, people, and things. People tend to crave this feeling, and Triple-A systems often reinforce it while reducing actual control. (Introduction)

Language Model for Dialogue Applications (LaMDA)—A family of conversational neural language models developed by Google. (Conclusion)

large learning models (LLMs)—Deep learning systems processing large quantities of unlabeled text in a self-supervised fashion; used in training generative AI systems. (Introduction)

limited-risk AI—Triple-A activity whose harm is related to its transparency obligations. According to the EU AIA, it should be required to routinely disclose its nonhuman nature. (Chapter 2)

loosely coupled systems—Charles Perrow's term for open and diverse architecture where changes in one module, section, or component hardly affect the other components in the system. This system is easy to scale and is robust. (Chapter 7)

machine behavior—An emerging academic discipline for studying what technological systems do in specific use cases and potentially in the context of human and organizational behavior. (Chapter 9)

machine learning (MA)—Triple-A systems that can change their behavior and adapt without following explicit instructions by using algorithms and statistical models to draw inferences from patterns in data. Engineers tend to prefer this term to artificial intelligence because it more accurately describes systems which, strictly speaking, are not intelligent. (Introduction, Chapter 5).

minimal-risk AI—Triple-A systems that do not require regulatory oversight because they do not harm people. (Chapter 1)

Moral Machine—An online experiment launched by the MIT Media Lab in 2016 to gather opinions on the life-or-death decisions a self-driving vehicle should make. (Introduction)

natural language processing (NLP) systems—The branch of artificial intelligence that focuses on teaching computers how to understand and replicate human language through text and speech. (Introduction)

negative bias—The tendency to accentuate fear and distaste rather than hope and curiosity. Triple-A systems can pick this up from data and favor people in the dominant culture. (Chapter 5)

open-source—Computer software that makes the source code public and allows users to freely modify and distribute it. (Chapter 3)

personal data—Information that can lead to the identification of a person or provide sensitive information to others. (Chapter 4)

predictive analytics—The use of data, statistical models, and machine learning to identify the likelihood of future outcomes. It can easily be misused with grave consequences for people who are singled out as future problems. (Chapter 2)

psychological safety—Amy Edmondson's term for organizational contexts where people can talk openly and freely without reprisal. (Chapter 8)

radical uncertainty—Times of great unpredictability in which small events can lead to large crises. (Chapter 2)

restraint bias—The tendency to overestimate the level of control people have over impulsive behaviors. This can lead people to sabotage their own interests when they encounter Triple-A systems. (Chapter 5)

risk intentionality—Ongoing determination, on the part of Triple-A system creators, to reduce risk to people—not just when convenient, but always. (Chapter 2)

risk thinking—Ron Dembo's term for the ability to take uncertainty into account, and thus to choose a flexible path that can respond to events as they unfold. Triple-A systems currently have limited risk thinking ability. (Chapter 1)

self-regulation—The practice of giving corporations or other entities sole responsibility for managing and mitigating the risks and damages related to their Triple-A systems. (Chapter 6)

social justice logic—The perspective of humanity. This logic prioritizes the social contract and ensures that technology does not infringe upon the rights of people, particularly vulnerable groups. (Chapter 1)

sociotechnical systems—Complex systems comprising of machines, people, and organizations. All Triple-A systems that interact with people are sociotechnical systems. (Introduction)

structural secrecy—Diane Vaughan's term for the innate tendency of government and business to keep activities hidden from view, even when there are benefits to revealing them. (Chapter 3)

tightly coupled systems—Charles Perrow's term for architectures that promote interdependence among their components and often isolation from outside connection. This makes them efficient and self-protective but less robust. (Chapter 7)

Triple-A systems—The full group of systems generally known as artificial intelligence, including algorithmic, autonomous, and automated systems. (Introduction)

unacceptable risk AI—Triple-A activity so potentially damaging to human beings that, according to the EU AIA, it should be prohibited. (Chapter 2)

warm data—Nora Bateson's term for transcontextual information about the interrelationships that connect elements of a complex system. (Chapter 5)

Acknowledgments

This book is an ethnographic work. The people interviewed for this book are friends, colleagues, and experts who care about and are invested in technology as much as in humanity. As they open their hearts, it is clear that the dilemmas involved with AI have the potential to tear them apart. Because these people chose to share their insider stories, we knew that their experiences would be valuable for others.

Thank you to Christina Ward and Matt Frika for helping shape the rough clay of our first draft. Your unique professional and personal experiences brought to bear the holistic, realistic, and human-centered view we needed to create incisive recommendations for our audience. Your networks of experts provided invaluable guidance and proof points.

Thank you to 3ric Johanson, Errol Cockfield, La'Kay Hodge, Ron Dembo, and Sean Gayle, who came in at just the right moments to knit together the strands of the manuscript when we needed it most.

Thank you to James (Jim) Wallace, who lived up to his "extroverted developer" title by sharing his deep technical expertise and history in the industry. He helped unpack the "why" behind a number of trends we explore in the book.

Thank you to Esther Dyson for the thought-provoking foreword.

Thank you to Steve Crandall, my anam cara, to Sukie Crandall, who held my hand through it all, and to both of you for your ongoing belief.

Thank you to people who gave generously of their time: Alan Chan, Alan Morrison, Anand Rao, Anthonio Pinheiro, Bran Ferren, Casey Cerretani, Catherine Booker, Cathy O'Neil, Christine Moser, Daniel Lim, Danny Hillis, Doug Rushkoff, Edmond Awad, Helen Greiner, Jim Gellert, John Sumser, John Sviokla, Kush Varshney, Lawrence Wilkinson, Lynn Cherny, Marc Rotenberg, Mark Anderson, Mauritz Kop, Michael Rosenbaum, Paul Gibbons, Peter Sloly, Ryan Carrier, and Tim Gilday.

Thank you to people who made a special effort to help us with *The AI Dilemma:* Adam Kahane, April Rinne, Astro Teller, Bill Isaacs, Dave Andre, David Bankston, David Lancefield, Doc and Joyce Searls, Dorie Clark, Emi Kolawole, Emma Asumeng, Errol Cockfield, Greg Sonbuchner, Guy Cohen, Helene Spierman, Ivo Stivoric, Iyad Rahman, Janet Logothetti, Jennifer Yales, Jerry Michalski, Jim O'Toole, John Battelle, John Markoff, Jonathan Askin, Kevin Clark, Mimi Yin, Peter Schwartz, Ron Dembo, Sarah Laszlo, Steven Levy, and Tymon Mattoszko.

Thank you to all those in tech who speak up publicly and inspire us: Anna Geiduschek, Daniel Sieradski, Frances Haugen, Jack Poulson, Joy Buolamwini, Leigh Honeywell, Meredith Whittaker, Sahil Talwar, Sean Parker, Timnit Gebru, Tristan Harris, and countless others.

Thank you to the academics whose work inspired and influenced our own: Adam Reich, Adele Diamond, Amy Edmondson, Ansgar Koene, Brian O'Keeffe, David C. Stark, Diane Vaughan, Jeffrey Schwartz, Jill Jensen, Knox Brown, Larry Au, Marka

Szabolcs, Matthew L. Jones, Michael Thaddeus, Peter Bearman, Peter Senge, Sharleen Smith, Shawn Van Every, Sheena Iyengar, Tom Igoe, Teresa Sharpe, Tim Devinney, Timothy Wu, Tom D'Aunno, and Shoshana Zuboff.

Thank you to everyone we have worked with at Berrett-Koehler: editor Neal Maillet, who first trusted that our ideas should be published; Jeevan Sivasubramaniam, Ashley Ingram, Edward Wade, Michael Crowley, Alexis Woodcock, David Marshall, and Steve Piersanti, among others. Thank you also to Westchester Publishing Services, especially Theresa Carcaldi, Angela Piliouras, and Karen Brogno, and to SAE Institute.

Thank you to the Women's Forum of New York for endowing Juliette while she was at Columbia University through the forum's wonderful education fund.

Thank you to the New York University Interactive Telecommunications Program [NYU ITP], where we taught a course related to the seven principles in this book. We thank all the students in the courses we have taught together on this and other subjects.

Thank you to the community of people who responded to our survey about the book's title, including Andrew Campbell, Ann Graham, Barry Vorster, Christopher Siddall, Hardin Tibbs, and Michael Schrage, among others.

Thank you again to those named here and to those we've unintentionally left out.

It takes a village: To all our friends from MusiquePlus, MuchMusic, BNN Bloomberg, particularly Jon Erlichman and Adena Ali, Bravo!, CityTV, CBC, CNN, CTV, MSNBC, BBC, NPR, Radio-Canada, especially Taffi Rosen and the irrepressible Marco Bresba; to my chosen family and the entire Chilton clan, Napier and Pat Collyns and the Collyns family, Amelia Rose Barlow and the Barlow family, DJ Guy Laliberte, Jean-Francois Bouchard, Daniel Lamarre, Dina Kaplan, Simon Carpenter et toute la famille Cirque du Soleil; to members of the Marshall Goldsmith 100, including Betsy Wills, David Peterson, Gregory Enialbert, Howie Jacobson, Lisa Nirell, Michael Gelb, Omran Matar, Rob Nail, Sally Helgesen, and others; Pip Coburn, Stephen Cruz, Wallace Moehlenbrok, Isabel and Scott Draves, Tom Shannon, Janet Thompson, Robert Talbot, and Josie Thomson; and to Art's family: Faith Florer, Elizabeth Kleiner, Constance Kleiner, Linda Heusser, and the Giards: Frances, Mike, EllaGrace, and Hazelee, who was born while *The AI Dilemma* was in copyedit.

Index

About the Authors

 Juliette Powell is an independent researcher, entrepreneur, and keynote speaker at the intersection of technology and business. Her consulting services focus on global strategy and scenarios related to AI and data, banking, mobile, retail, social gaming, and responsible technology. She has delivered live commentary on Bloomberg, BNN, NBC, CNN, ABC, and BBC and presentations at institutions like The Economist, Harvard, and MIT. She works with such organizations as Reuters, the United Nations, Warner Brothers, l'Union des Banques Suisses, Microsoft, The Red Cross, Cirque du Soleil, IBM, and the World Bank Group.

Juliette's previous book is *33 Million People in the Room: How to Create, Influence, and Run a Successful Business with Social Networking* (Financial Times Press, 2009). She was a cofounder with Intel Labs of the research network WeTheData. *The AI Dilemma* is based in part on her research conducted at Columbia University. Powell is a faculty member at New York University's Interactive Telecommunications Program and the founding partner of Kleiner Powell International (KPI), kleinerpowell.com.

Art Kleiner is a writer, editor, and entrepreneur with a background in technology and business culture. He writes, speaks and consults on topics related to machine, organizational, and human behavior, the neuroscience of leadership, content strategy, and the strategies and insights needed in business to manage complex dilemmas. He is also an experienced facilitator and lecturer in scenario thinking and organizational learning. His books include *The Age of Heretics: A History of the Radical Thinkers Who Reinvented Corporate Management* (Warren Bennis Books/Jossey-Bass, 1996 and 2018); *Who Really Matters: The Core Group Theory of Power, Privilege and Success* (Random House, 2003); and (with Jeffrey Schwartz and Josie Thomson) *The Wise Advocate: The Inner Voice of Strategic Leadership* (Columbia University Business Press, 2019). He is a faculty member at New York University's Interactive Telecommunications and Interactive Media Programs in Tisch School of the Arts.

Between 2005 and 2020, Kleiner was the editor-in-chief of the award-winning management magazine *Strategy+Business,* and a director at Booz Allen Hamilton and PwC. Before that, he was editorial director of the best-selling *Fifth Discipline Fieldbook* series with Peter Senge et al. He was also an editor at the *Whole Earth Catalog,* where he oversaw coverage of computers and business. He was one of the first people to write about the internet and its effect on people. Kleiner has a degree in journalism from the University of California at Berkeley. He is editor-in-chief at Kleiner Powell International (KPI), kleinerpowell.com.

Dear reader,

Thank you for picking up this book and welcome to the worldwide BK community! You're joining a special group of people who have come together to create positive change in their lives, organizations, and communities.

What's BK all about?

Our mission is to connect people and ideas to create a world that works for all.

Why? Our communities, organizations, and lives get bogged down by old paradigms of self-interest, exclusion, hierarchy, and privilege. But we believe that can change. That's why we seek the leading experts on these challenges—and share their actionable ideas with you.

A welcome gift

To help you get started, we'd like to offer you a **free copy** of one of our bestselling ebooks:

www.bkconnection.com/welcome

When you claim your **free ebook**, you'll also be subscribed to our blog.

Our freshest insights

Access the best new tools and ideas for leaders at all levels on our blog at ideas.bkconnection.com.

Sincerely,

Your friends at Berrett-Koehler

Certified

Corporation